Re:Thinking Mission

Re:Thinking Mission

Simon Cozens

Wide Margin Books

Re:Thinking Mission
Author: Simon Cozens
© 2018-2020 Simon Cozens

Version: report@master-3ef502f*

Table of Contents

FOREWORD

A large portion of this book was written during coronavirus lockdown in the UK. The combined effect of the pressure of time, the inability to access to needed resources, and general decreased productivity due to disruption means that the final manuscript is not as complete as I would have liked.

In particular, a planned chapter on trends in the global church has been cut down and merged into other sections; I was not able to adequately contextualise the very important area of diaspora missiology, but have instead provided links to further references; and I had planned to analyse examples of successful technological innovations in mission.

Perhaps a future edition will be able to restore these missing areas, but for now, I hope that these omissions will not significantly affect the reader's ability to follow my lines of argument and come to the same conclusions.

1

The Road We're On

CHAPTER ONE

Unpacking our assumptions

It started with an amazing question. "If we were going to start again, as a church planting mission agency, with the same goal of reaching the unreached, what would we do?" Our agency, WEC International, recently celebrated one hundred years since its founding. A hundred years is a long time in mission, and the world is a very different place than it was a hundred years ago. Should we still be doing the same things?

WEC has reinvented itself a number of times throughout those hundred years. Still, each new milestone brings with it the opportunity - perhaps even the necessity - to reappraise what has gone before, to take stock of where we are, to critically evaluate our practice, and to look to the future. In what areas of our operation and organisation are we "running on autopilot", continuing with received wisdom and ways of doing things from a bygone generation? Is our current wineskin still appropriate to hold the new wine of the Spirit, and if not what would a new "wineskin" look like? What should we hold on to from the past and what do we need to reconceptualize for the future? In other words, do the assumptions by which we operate still make sense in today's world?

To answer these questions, we must first investigate what our assumptions are. The tricky thing about assumptions is that they are assumed; they form part of our worldview to the extent that we don't notice them. And so we will begin our attempt to rethink mission, in this chapter and the one that follows, by making explicit some of the things we hold implicit. In this chapter, we will unpack some of the assumptions in our research question and within the context of our mission agency; in the next, we will look more broadly at the missiological basis on which we operate. Clarifying how we think about these assumptions will shape the way that we respond.

A CHURCH PLANTING MISSION?

WEC defines its activity explicitly in terms of "reaching people" amongst "unreached peoples" - essentially pioneer evangelism, often done through the process of planting churches. So before we even examine the question, the very first assumption that we find is the assumption that having a primary focus on pioneer evangelism and church planting constitutes a legitimate expression of mission. Should an organisation with a focus on pioneer evangelism and church planting even exist at all?

One could argue that if we are completely rethinking mission practice from the ground up, we should also question the assumption of an agency retaining this kind of focus. (And indeed others have done so.)[1] But this is one assumption that I have chosen to take on trust, even if this means that we come to conclusions about the future of mission which are not universal and general, but which are instead specific to expressions of mission like our own which prioritize pioneer ministry. This is my own conviction, and it's important to have that clearly on the record.

---

1. See Wati Longchar, et al., ed., 2007, *They Left by Another Road: Rerouting Mission and Ecumenism in Asia*, Chiangmai: CCA.

This is not simply because I would find it politically difficult to suggest that my own organisation should disband and start doing something completely different! If I genuinely believed that was what God was saying to us, I would not hesitate to recommend it. There are two reasons why I have chosen to accept the church planting focus as a basic foundation, rather than as a topic for discussion, even if the means, the structures and the practices are to change. These reasons operate on two separate levels.

On the first level, I do not believe that a focus on pioneer church planting negates a commitment to a wider, more holistic mission, nor does it imply that other forms of mission and ministry are unimportant. The Evangelical community has long vacillated over the question of priority between evangelism and social action, but gradually, and due in large part to the influence of missiology from the majority world, the Evangelical understanding of mission has moved towards an integral position.[2] Indeed, whatever the theological arguments on both sides, for the emerging generation of missionaries, the balance between evangelism and social action is simply not a live issue. Regardless of their intellectual understanding of mission, within their lived theology, the primacy of social action has won the day.

Within that context, an assumption of missionary activity that focuses on evangelism and church planting seems strangely old-fashioned. To answer that, I would take the position that authentic pioneer evangelism and church planting *requires* involvement in other activities; "there can be no authentic evangelism apart from a living testimony to the

---

2.   See René Padilla, 2002, "Integral Mission and its Historical Development", in T. Chester (ed.) *Justice, Mercy and Humility*, Carlisle: Paternoster, pp. 42-58.

transforming power of the Gospel in action".[3] Of course, I am
aware that the word "authentic" is doing a lot of work in
those previous sentences. It is certainly possible for someone
to evangelise and minister solely on a spiritual level, and to
meaningfully bring the Gospel to others while shying away
from involvement in social transformation, and I am sure that
those doing so would regard what they are doing as "authentic evangelism".

But evangelism is not merely the intellectual transfer of
knowledge about salvation. It must be expressed in relationship. The problem with the discussion around the balance between social action and evangelism is that, like many distinctions, it is easy to draw in a theoretical framework, but has
a way of becoming blurred and messy in the testing-ground
of praxis. Another assumption, which I suggest needs no attempt at justification, is that mission is carried out through
the medium of love. Love necessitates deep enagement in
the lives of those you love. The struggles of people you love
resonate with you, involve you emotionally, move you to the
extent that they become your own struggles – whether that is
a struggle for food and economic security, for safety in con-
ditions of conflict, for liberation from situations of injustice,
or for protection from natural disasters caused by a changing
global climate. Church planting cannot be done at a "critical
distance" from the lives of those we live and work amongst.

So if we see church planting as an integral activity with
multiple social and relational dimensions, why speak of church
planting at all, then? If what we *mean* by church planting
is not "purely" church planting, then there is an argument
for changing the terminology to reflect this: should we not

3.   Andrew Kirk, 1999, *What Is Mission?*, London: Darton, Longman and Todd, . 57.

use the language of "integral mission", "integral church planting", or similar instead? In a sense, language used by organisation such as a mission agency has two audiences: it is
used to communicate with those inside the organisation and
also with those outside. So long as those inside are aware
of the expectations of integrality in their mission practice,
(which will need to be communicated well both by example
and by word: shared stories of transformative and holistic
church plants, and clear statements of what is meant underlying the umbrella term "church planting") the use of a term
like "church planting" can have useful external significance
in differentiating WEC as an agency which works integrally
through church planting.

But should that even be a factor? When an organisation
says that it chooses to use church planting as its focus for integral mission, does that not explicitly prioritize church planting as a form of ministry? Perhaps so, but I would respond
that creating a focus around a particular form of ministry is,
in and of itself, both a legitimate and indeed a *necessary* expression of mission. For this, we need to answer the question
on the second level.

Mission is always an exercise in partnership. It is common these days to speak of mission as a partnership with
God, indeed one in which God is in the driving seat; but it
is equally an exercise of human partnership as well. In New
Testament models of mission, both those of Jesus and of the
apostles, we see the ubiquity of partnership - teams, supporters, networks of relationships, obligations and accountability.
The "independent missionary", to the extent that such a concept is valid, may be *organisationally* independent, but they
are rarely, if ever, relationally so.

When I speak generally about mission "organisations",
then, I am not just referring to the agencies and societies of
the Western cross-cultural mission movement. I am simply
talking about any vehicles for mission partnership, at whatever level of administrative or bureaucratic sophistication.
This would include a group of friends or a church uniting
to commission one of their own as a missionary, right up to
a large multinational corporate structure. Each of these "organisations" revolves around partnership based on a shared
commitment. For some, the shared commitment is a common
project, or interest in a geographical area. For others, it will
involve a shared theological or denominational commitment.
Yet others will band together on the basis of personal rela-
tionalships or the charismatic attraction of a founding leader
- and often suffer a crisis of identity for it when handing on to
another generation, sometimes having to rediscover or invent
a different kind of shared basis to maintain continuity.

The mission "organisation", then, in the sense that I have
used the word above, is not so much a deliberately justifiable
feature of mission practice but an unavoidable fact of human
life. Practically speaking, we cannot partner with everyone.
Human beings form themselves into manageable sized groups
to bring order and simplicity to a complex world. Just as there
is no such thing as a truly independent missionary, there is
no such thing as a truly general mission organisation, nor can
there be. Of course, there is a wider sense of partnership in
which we wish to see mission organisations work together as
one body across the divisions of their distinctions; there is the
wider sense in which all expressions of Christian mission are
part of the same body of Christ.

But on a local and operational level, specialization is the basis on which we form partnerships for mission. That is something for which we need make no apologies. Continuing to take up Paul's metaphor of the body gives us useful vocabulary here: the hand and the eye work together within the body, but the hand does not need to do the work of the eye and vice versa. The cells which make up the eye will be different to those which make up the hand, yet they are one body. Within a wider unity, there is particular specialization. And once we accept that, and so long as we are aware that specialization is not *exclusive* but merely provides a focus, I would argue that the choice of specialization is essentially arbitrary; there is no point in asking the eye *why* it is an eye, why it is so committed to seeing, and what it plans to do about grasping. If we were not one body part, we should surely be another, and similar questions would apply.

The context of this current investigation, then, is an organisation which has banded together around both shared values and a shared commitment to a particular form of ministry. The efficacy and viability of church planting as a choice of ministry form is an important question; but in another sense, it is besides the point. As we all do, I write from a position of commitment, and to a community of commitment. So long as we are content that this commitment is one which forms a part of the body, that it is within the boundaries of something that we can call "mission" - and that is something we will examine in the next chapter - then we should be equally content to move forward on the basis of this commitment.

But this does serve to narrow the scope of our investigation. We are not seeking a grand solution to the future of *all kinds* of mission; instead, we are looking for what are appropriate models for church planting ministry in today's context. Others will need to do similar work to explore what is appropriate for their communities.

WHAT HAPPENS WHEN WE TALK ABOUT THE "UNREACHED"

Even within this scope, though, there are some more important assumptions underlying our initial question which do require more nuance. We are looking for the most appropriate ways to "reach the unreached", as well as the most appropriate organisational vehicles and forms to support this kind of activity. What this means is that we are assuming that there are people who are "unreached", and that it is our job to "reach" them.

We will come back to look specifically at the assumptions surrounding the "unreached" soon, but before we do so, notice how we have already, almost subconsciously, framed the discussion in linear, instrumentalist terms: we are assuming that there is a problem, and that we know what the problem is (the problem is that there are people groups in which there is no self-sustaining church); and we are assuming that our role is to involve ourselves in solving that problem. That is our *task*.

There are, of course, some dangers in conceptualizing mission as a task that we need to complete. We will deconstruct the more subtle dangers, and point towards possible alternate conceptions, in the next chapter. For now, and accepting for a moment the idea that mission is a task which "we do", the most obvious danger is the danger of forming a narrow definition of the "task" and then allowing that definition to determine, rather than to inform, praxis. We can proceed too quickly from goal to outcomes to strategy, and such a process drives us inexorably towards a reductionistic understanding of mission. When we know what the task of mission is, then mission becomes a matter of "finishing the task", and resources - particularly money - become prioritized in service of achieving a measurable goal.

Measurability does give focus and definition to a task. But whenever something can be measured - hospital waiting times, students' test results, unemployment figures - people are often tempted towards "output distortions" in two directions. The first is called "hitting the target but missing the point". A school which is being ranked alongside other schools on exam results will face the temptation of "teaching to the test", coaching pupils on how to pass exams more than developing a deep understanding of the subject. A call centre which measures efficiency in calls per hour will find that workers try to keep calls short, even if customers do not have their questions satisfactorily answered - and anyone who was called such a centre will know that a task-focused emphasis on results comes at the expense of meaningful relationship!

If mission becomes defined as a race against time or a task to be fulfilled, then reaching the unreached or engaging the unengaged can (unwittingly, of course, but driven by a sense of urgency) become a box-ticking exercise. Engagement is done quickly and superficially, resources are rearranged to more "needy" areas as soon as progress hits an arbitrary definition, and strategy becomes driven by a one-size-fits-all approach that prioritizes absolute and global principles over local contextual cues. None of this is intentional; but it happens.

It is worth reminding ourselves how God goes about His mission. God is not efficient as we understand efficiency, nor

does He seem to operate according to our sense of urgency
and need for constant progress. Indeed, His salvation story
unfurls at a glacially slow pace. There is setback, reversion
and failure along the way. "Forty years of national migration through the wilderness, three generations of the united
monarchy... nineteen kings of Israel and twenty kings of Ju-
dah, the hosts of the prophets and priests, the experience
of exile and restoration - isn't this rather a slow and costly
way for God to let his people know the covenant relationship
between God and man?... God walks 'slowly' because he is
love. If he is not love he could have gone much faster."[4]

The second distortion caused by a narrow and measurable
definition of "the task" is the temptation to fiddle the metrics
- changing the definition to get the numbers that one wants.
(According to the British economist Charles Goodhart, "Any
observed statistical regularity will tend to collapse once pressure is placed upon it for control purposes.")[5] The motivation
for the recent urge to clearly define unreached people groups
has been mixed: for one thing, as a means of mobilization; as
another, to draw attention to the amount of mission resources
devoted to areas where the church is already "established"
in comparison to areas where people have never heard the
Gospel; and then, more recently, as part of a theology of
closure, seeking to "finish the task" of mission.[6]

This is not the place to assess those motivations, ex-
cept to mention that different groups have given different
emphasis to each of these reasons. This has led to thinking around Unreached People Groups accordingly becoming

4. Kosuke Koyama, 1979, *Three Mile An Hour God*, London: SCM Press, p. 7.
5. Charles Goodhart, 1981, "Problems of Monetary Management: The U.K. Experience". In
    Courakis, Anthony S. (ed.). *Inflation, Depression, and Economic Policy in the West*, pp. 111–
    146.
6. (See Eschlemann, 2010)

bogged down with definitional arguments:[7] does a group need a certain percentage of Christians (or Evangelicals) to be considered reached? Is a group demarcated by some combination of linguistic, ethnic, caste, occupational, geographical, or social lines? (And is any particular combination less arbitrary than any other?)

Additional concepts such as "unengaged", "under-engaged", "frontier", "least-reached" actually provide *less* clarity rather than more. A diversity of definitions and statistical measures means that organisations may quote entirely different statistics about the same groups as they are working from subtly different and incommensurable evidence bases: the Joshua Project counts 6571 unreached people groups in the world, the IMB count 6827, and the World Christian Database lists 4219. Does this really help to give "precision" and "definition" to the missionary task?

At the same time, we must be careful around the idea of a prioritized scale of "reachedness." Perhaps it is better to avoid language such as "least reached", as this communicates a sense of greater priority when all people are equally precious to God. We need to keep in mind that His ways are not our ways.

One missionary candidate heading for Spain told me that hearing Spain talked about as a "reached" country (by one organisation's definition) made him feel that his work - and what he believed to be his call

---

7. As noted by Dave Datema (2016, "Defining"Unreached": A Short History", *International Journal of Frontier Missiology*, 33:2, 45-71) and R W Lewis (2016,"Losing Sight of the Frontier Mission Task: What's Gone Wrong with the Demographics?", *International Journal of Frontier Missiology*, 35:1, 5-15).

from God - was being judged as illegitimate and unimportant.

At the same time, we need to bear in mind the fact that the vast majority of missionary activity is directed to areas of the world which have significant Evangelical populations. Foreign missionary activity in these areas can, of course, bolster and support local churches; but equally likely, they can breed a culture of dependency and discourage local believers from taking their place in God's mission. "A reduction of foreign missionaries and money in an evangelized country may sometimes be necessary to facilitate the national church's growth in self-reliance and to release resources for unevangelized areas."[8] Hence, some degree of prioritization of activity is necessary, not just for the sake of the "unreached" but *also for the sake of the "reached"*.

BEYOND MANAGERIAL MISSIOLOGY

For some, the entire concept of "reaching the unreached" or developing a "missions strategy" is theologically and missiologically problematic, to the point of being unredeemable. Padilla, Escobar and others have brought an important critique to the Western mission movement's obsession with strategy, numbers, and the use of "managerial" methods in the exercise of mission.[9] Escobar argues against the use of the

---

8.   Lausanne Congress on World Evangelism, 1974, *Lausanne Covenant*, section 9.
9.   See, particularly, Samuel Escobar, 2000, "Evangelical Missiology: Peering into the Future", in W. D. Taylor (ed.), *Global Missiology for the 21st Century*, Grand Rapids, MI: Baker Academic.

"quantitative approach" to mission, which reduces missionary activity to a "linear task that is translated into logical steps to be followed in a process of management by objectives."

This is a critique which we need to carefully hear, and where necessary, repent and change our direction. For example, the conceptualization of mission primarily in terms of task rather than relationship is a symptom of this managerial trend in mission thinking. It *is* theologically unacceptable to reduce *people* to numbers or to see them as "targets" or "objects" of mission rather than primarily as the recipients of God's love; indeed, theologians such as Koyama would describe it as demonic. It *is* hegemonistic and hubristic to attempt to form overarching "strategies" for world evangelisation. We will see later that the reconceptualization of mission as God's mission, the *missio dei* principle, is an important corrective to the understanding of mission as a thing which we can humanly determine and control.

But we must also be aware that some of the distinctions between Western, "strategic" missiology and non-Western "relational" missiology are perhaps differences of emphasis brought about by vocabulary. Such choices of vocabulary matter in as much as they go some way towards *reflecting* our mental framework of what mission is: the use of military metaphors in mission (including the term "strategy" - from the Greek "strategos", military general - and, arguably, the word "mission" itself[10]) being a case in point. This, too, is a critique that we need to hear and understand. And yet, the Lakoffian claim that choices of vocabulary and metaphor *determine* our subconscious attitudes towards a subject is far

---

10. See *Consultation Statement*, Consultation on Mission Language and Metaphors, Fuller Theological Seminary, 1-3 June 2000.

from proven; meaning evolves, and etymology is not destiny. Anyone who has shared the Gospel in a broken second or third language will know that the fragile and fallible choice of words aim to serve as vehicles for the heart intentions of love behind them.

And so it is that any time you ask a missionary - Western or non-Western - the question "What do you actually do?", you are asking them to enunciate a methodology, which a Western person may well refer to as a strategy. The strategy may be to spend time with people; to seek out and take part in the way that God is moving within a community; to simply be salt and light and a witness to the Kingdom of God - or, of course, it may be to focus one's attention on particular people in particular places for particular reasons. The mere *creation* of strategy, in itself, is not the sinful part of the equation; what is important is the content of such a strategy, and whether or not we make our strategies into our idols. "Resourcefulness... must be theologically judged and contextualized in order to become genuinely resourceful. Resourcefulness must then be crucified. When it is resurrected it will become a 'theologically-baptized resourcefulness'... In the perspective of mission together in the six continents we urgently need ecumenical meditation on the theology of crucified resourcefulness."[11]

In Acts 16, we see Paul making deliberate and systematic progress in evangelising the province of Asia Minor, working clockwise from Antioch through Ephesus and then into Bithynia. He had an aim in mind which he initially followed, up until the point at which the Holy Spirit would no longer allow him to do so. Instead, Paul was directed across the

11. Kosuke Koyama, 1979, *No Handle on the Cross*, Maryknoll: Orbis Books, p. 5.

Aegean, where he was led to a woman living in Philippi - who was an economic migrant from Asia Minor.

Paul's priorities for the people of Asia Minor were fulfilled, but only once he was prepared, in humble submission to the direction of the Spirit, to lay down his strategy and respond to the leading of God. Mission which is to go beyond the managerial model requires two elements to be in place: an operational methodology - that is, having a way which we set out to go - and a spiritual and relational flexibility - being prepared to be taken out of our way.

In my own missionary journey, I had to learn to temper strategy with relationship. We arrived as church planters with a clear idea of what we were going to do and how we were going to approach establishing a new church - but the strategy did not survive first contact with the mission field, as within a week God had clearly brought a number of people into our lives who did not fit into our plan! We could have ploughed on with our ideas, but to do so would have been to clearly ignore both the people and the Lord. So we had to drastically adapt our methods to reflect the relationships that God had prepared for us.

But the fact that the strategy was interrupted and redirected does not negate the value of having a strategy in the first place. Rather, it was because we had moved out on the basis of our strategy that we came into the position where we *could* be interrupted, in much the same way that Paul needed to follow his systematic journey all the way to Bythnia before he could be directed across to Philippi.

I am assuming, then, that underlying any "managerial language" in the way that we discuss what new forms of mission are going to look like is a recognition that this is only

the first element, the operational methodology - the thing that
you do until God interrupts you and takes you elsewhere. I
am also assuming that missionaries and mission communities
taking up these suggested forms do so on the basis of the
second element, a sensitivity to the leading of the Spirit and
a readiness to jettison any strategy, however well-meaning,
when love requires it.

KEEPING THE BALANCE

Seeking to "reach the unreached" leaves us with a difficult balance to maintain: on the one hand, we see that voicing
a priority for the unreached encourages cross-cultural missionary activity in parts of the world where there is little to
no effective local Christian witness, and discourages "step-
ping on the toes" of growing and capable local churches; on
the other, however, we wish to avoid buying wholesale into
a quantitative understanding of mission which reduces "the
unreached" to mere statistical measures and strategic targets.
On the third hand, (for the body of Christ has many hands)
we recognise that mission is not ours to control, and that
God's calling sometimes takes us in directions that we did not
anticipate. How do we hold these three elements in tension?

Looking back over WEC's own history, we find that,
paradoxically, a focus on the unreached has actually helped
us in this. By combining a clear focus on areas where Christ is
not known with a sense of generous hospitality towards what
we recognise as God's leading, we have been able to incubate
and develop "side projects" while simultaneously "keeping
the main thing the main thing." A prime example of this is the
Christian Literature Crusade, which began life inside WEC
but was then "released" as a separate ministry.

Another factor which has helped with this has been a relatively fluid definition of "the unreached". Rather than using strict ethnolinguistic categories (which, it can argued, reflect an outdated and essentialist understanding of anthropology[12]), WEC understands the term "unreached people" as referring to

> An identifiable people group in which there is no indigenous community of believers with adequate numbers, resources, or commitment to evangelize itself.

> While WEC's primary focus is reaching ethnolinguistically defined unreached people groups, 'groups of people' with a common affinity who have no access to the gospel unless someone crosses barriers may also be considered as unreached.

This wider definition has enabled WEC ministries both with settled and diaspora people groups but has also encompassed drug addicts (Betel), children at risk (Rainbows of Hope), and refugees.

Additionally, the definition is expressed in qualitative rather than a quantitative measures; we talk about the *commitment* of a people to evangelise themselves, which is not something that can be assessed from statistical measures in a database, but requires subjective evaluation of the field situation. It is these subjective elements which keep our mission focused on the human, rather than mechanical.

This idea of reaching a people group up until the point they have a commitment to evangelize themselves is more time consuming, more costly, and more difficult than a sim-

---

12. Tite Tiénou. 2016, "Reflections on Michael A. Rynkiewich's"Do Not Remember the Former Things"". *International Bulletin of Missionary Research* 40:4, pp. 318–324.

ple numbers-based approach. It has no clear indicators of
progress. It creates uncertainty and offers no guarantees of
success; there may be resistance and reversion along the way.
It is also vague and hard to measure. But it is precisely because mission must be done through an attitude of humility,
based within the local context, and taking place at the slow
and costly "speed of love", that mission must focus on meaningful and subjective engagement.

SUMMARY

We have begun our investigation by looking "behind the
question" at some of the assumptions at play when we ask the
question within the context of our organisation. Even though
we have ultimately affirmed these assumptions, the process
of investigating them has produced a clearer understanding
of the context of rethinking mission.

We have discovered that we are seeking to answer questions about the future of mission from the context of an
organisation of people who have banded together with a
methodological focus on church planting, and a focus and
distinct - but not exclusive - emphasis on and priority towards
the "unreached". We've also noted that when we say "church
planting", we're referring to it as a way to give focus to what
is overall an integral understanding of mission, and we've
noted that in order to do that, we need to share stories and
give clear guidance about what we expect integral church
planting to look like.

We have considered some of the problems that a priority
towards the "unreached" can entail. As a result of this, we do
not see the "unreached" as part of a metric in a race to "finish
the task" or to chart progress, nor do we want to suggest that
mission alongside existing churches or in "evangelized areas"

is less legitimate or less necessary. But we use it to state our position of commitment, and one of our bases for partnership, which is that we wish to work to establish churches where there is little or no Christian witness.

On that basis, we will be using statistics and case studies of "unreached peoples" in this survey, but with the above caveats in mind. Looking at signficant clusters of unreached peoples is not an end in itself, a *substitute* for theological and missiological reflection, but it can be a basis on which to begin such reflection. Investigating the context of the world today can provide a rich source of examples: examples of circumstances which might necessitate new forms or directions in ministry, and examples which give us a fresh perspective and inspire creative thought about missional possibilities.

A focus on the unreached is, then, a force for organisational cohesion and a driver for missional creativity more than it is something that can be directly applied to create an overarching strategy; we see it as a good servant but recognise its dangers as a bad master. An organisation which seeks to reach the unreached will encourage and direct resources towards this focus, researching and highlighting opportunities and gaps in the missionary movement, but will, like Paul, remain sensitive to the leading of the Holy Spirit for changes of direction and strategy.

CHAPTER TWO
What is mission?

We have, to this point, been using the word "mission" in a loose sense. But one persistent discussion in the world of mission, particularly over the last fifty years, has been surrounding the definition of "mission" itself. What do we mean when we talk about "mission"?

For a long time, the mission movement was sufficiently privileged and sufficiently self-confident that questions about the fundamental nature of mission were seen as a distraction from mission practice - mission agencies and individuals had a "good enough" working understanding of what they thought mission was and what it involved, (perhaps expressed in pithy statements about "bringing the Gospel to all nations") and they were happy to leave the precise theological reflection to the missiologists.

But the "time of testing" in which we find ourselves "calls for a new understanding of mission."[1] As we will examine in chapters four and five, the world and the church have profoundly changed. Some of these changes directly challenge existing missions structures, which have predominantly been developed to suit Western models. The rise of the global church, the decline of the Western church with its Christendom model of church and mission, post-colonial reflection

---

1. Bosch, D., 1991. *Transforming mission: Paradigm shifts in theology of mission*. Maryknoll, NY: Orbis, 366.

and repentance, and changing geopolitical power structures (to name but a few factors) mean that this search for a new understanding of mission is not simply a theoretical one, but is having practical impact on missionaries and mission agencies' praxis and self-definition.

In one sense, the answer to the question is simple. Mission is sending. Its root is the Latin *mittere*, used to translate the Greek terms *aposteilo* and *pempo*. Someone who is sent is an emissary: an *apostolos* in Greek, or *missus* or *legatus* in Latin. Barnabas is called an *apostle* in Acts 14:14 because he is a sent-one, doing the work of a *missionary*.

We see many "sendings" in Scripture. Wright describes seven instances of God sending in the Old Testament.[2] In the New Testament, the Father sends the Son, then sends the Spirit. And the Son sends the Apostles: "*sicut misit me Pater et ego mitto vos*", said Jesus: "as the Father sent me, so I send you." (John 20:21) In this passage, the sending of the Son by the Father is paralleled in the sending of the disciples by the Son; we are sent to continue the ministry of Jesus, under his orders and sovereignty. "Rather than operating on the basis of marketing surveys or mere human strategizing, the contemporary church therefore needs to subordinate itself consciously to the salvation-historical purposes Jesus seeks to pursue in our day."[3]

And yet this leaves us with significant questions about *what* is done, *how* it is done, *where* it is done, and *by whom* it is done.

---

2.   Wright, 2017, *The Mission of God's People*, 203-209.
3.   Kösterberger and O'Brien, 2001, *Salvation to the Ends of the Earth*, Downers Grove, IL: Apollos, 225.

PROBLEMATIZING MISSION: GLOBAL AND LOCAL

The first problem is what we consider to be the scope of mission, and how mission is delineated. Where does mission happen, and what does it look like? As we have mentioned, once upon a time, the answer to these questions was easy: mission is going to other parts of the world to share the Gospel. But recent developments, both social and theological, have caused the definition to widen. A growing global multiculturalism and urbanisation, a Western post-modern and post-Christendom insecurity about evangelism, and the growing realisation that mission is joining in God's activity in all its varied forms have all contributed to the scope of "mission" being ever further extended.

Perhaps following Stephen Neill's dictum that "if everything is mission, then nothing is mission", many Western cross-cultural mission agencies have attempted to push back and re-emphasise a more limited definition of mission - perhaps to justify their own priorities and their continued existence. But they seem to be facing a losing battle.

"My church says that they're involved in mission because they fund one or two overseas projects, run a lot of short term trips and 'do mission' locally. But that's not what mission is." - UK missionary

This missionary had a clear understanding of "what mission is" - mission means supporting long-term, overseas, cross-cultural ministry operations, normally facilitated by an external organisation or agency. And yet she found herself frustrated that her church is operating from a quite different definition of mission: one that is primarily about local ministry, but with short-term foreign engagement organised and operated by the local church itself. This is not an unrepresentative position in Western churches, and Rollin Grams explicitly ties this turn towards localism with a more "holistic" understanding of mission:

> I think that the main reason for questioning foreign missions in Evangelical circles is the loss of an understanding of what the mission of the Church is. Mission has become everything, not only everything that churches do but everything that individual Christians can do. Why go abroad when there is plenty of work to do 'right here'? Why do that work when there is other work to do as well? Thus, we need to clarify what the mission of the Church is and to articulate this mission with respect to the Church, not just good works or ideals or causes and the like.[4]

Similarly, Mantenga and Gold, in their international survey of mission motivation, arrive at a maximalist definition of mission, where, in a sense, everything *is* mission because God is involved in everything:

> Whether it is related to personal salvation or social action, locally or across some sort of sociocultural barrier, in a part-time capacity or as a professional career... a Christian belief in God should promote action that makes a positive impact, which therefore should be considered mission."[5]

There is a merit in this holism. "Slowly, and somewhat painfully, mission is becoming uncoupled from its association with the previous Western movement of evangelism and church planting and being redefined to cover the calling of the Church, at

---

4. Rollin Grams, 2018, *Ten Challenges To Resolve in Western Missions in the 21st Century*, https://bibleandmission.blogspot.com/2018/06/the-21-st-century-is-well-upon-usand.html
5. Mantega and Gold, 2016, *Mission in Motion*, Pasadena, CA: William Carey Library, 70.

every level and in every place, to be part of God's mission in the world... Mission is quite simply, though profoundly, what the Christian community is sent to do, beginning right where it is located."[6]

The operational understanding of mission, particularly dominant in Western churches, is therefore no longer about sending people to foreign lands to plant churches, but refers to participating in all that God is involved with in the world, beginning where the church finds itself. But another way to say this is that God's mission has given the church so much to do "at home" that there is less time and impetus to focus on mission "over there". As humans, it is always easier to prioritize what is before one's eyes over what is happening miles away. Similarly, it is always easier to prioritize what we feel comfortable doing over what we find difficult; in a post-Christendom culture where the church is less confident about its right and responsibility to evangelise, Western churches may find themselves more involved in mercy and justice projects, which are easier to justify both to itself and to the outside world.

But this is not purely a Western phenomenon, as Mantega and Gold point out. They quote Eastern European, South American, East African, Asian and Indian respondents alike recognizing "a more general locus for mission" and refusing to draw a distinction between global and local mission.[7] Indeed, from a postcolonial perspective, church leaders in contexts which were historically the *recipients* of foreign cross-cultural mission work expressed the view that mission began with taking responsibility for ministering to that local con-

6. (Kirk, 1999:24)
7. Mantega and Gold, 2016, *Mission in Motion*, Pasadena, CA: William Carey Library, 59.

text, and that this *local* mission was something that they were better equipped for than foreign missionaries were. "Whatever mission looked like in their context, as done by foreign missionaries, is now something they need to do themselves." Cross-cultural mission is then seen as an archaic remnant of the old order of mission.

This presents us with a conundrum. If we accept that all of these elements - global and local, social action and evangelism - are equally part of God's mission for the church; if we reject the doctrine of salt water, the idea that there is something intrinsically more spiritually significant about mission which is done in a different country; then surely we have no grounds to criticize a church body which prioritizes local expressions of mission. But at the same time, we cannot help feeling that something is missing. How do we resolve this tension?

First, mission is certainly being involved in what God is doing, wherever He is doing it, and He is certainly at work everywhere in the world. One can indeed do mission anywhere. But mission also has an intrinsic direction of travel, and this direction of travel is always "outwards". Mission from Jerusalem can be done in Jerusalem - Wright points out that the disciples were apostles in Jerusalem, and so being "sent" does not *necessitate* geographical travel[8] - but at the same time it cannot end there: "the city is the source of the gospel message for the whole world. But the word of the Lord is no longer tied to the holy city; it *must* go out from Jerusalem."[9] Kösterberger and O'Brian further describe how

---

8. Wright, 2017, *The Mission of God's People*, 212.
9. Kösterberger and O'Brien, 2001, *Salvation to the Ends of the Earth*, Downers Grove, IL: Apollos, 136, emphasis mine.

the new outward impetus in mission after Jesus' resurrection was a fulfilment of Isaiah's prophecy that "the Law will go out from Zion, the word of the LORD from Jerusalem" (2:3). "The ongoing powerful advance of the word of God is a central theme of Acts which may have its antecedents in this Old Testament prophecy."

Much has been made of the fact that the command of Jesus to "go" in Matthew 28:19 is not actually an imperative command but a modifying participle: "as you go." Making disciples is the main verb, and it is to be done "along the way." But another way to put this is that "going" is *assumed*. Unpopular though it may be, churches must be gently encouraged that although one can indeed do mission by "going" "across the street", this must be placed in the context of the outward unfolding of God's word towards the ends of the earth.

Second, discussions around the locus of mission can quickly denegerate into conversations about need and priority. Churches will argue that they do not need to go over "there" when there is so much need "here". Missionaries will counter with arguments about other parts of the world being needier or having less "access to the Gospel". But these arguments are becoming harder and harder to make; there is clearly as much, or more, "need" for evangelisation in Western Europe than in many parts of East Africa, South America, or South Asia. Still, missionaries from the West particularly may yet be unwilling or unable to accept that their home countries are, by any metric, just as spiritually needy or "unreached" as traditionally mission-receiving nations. Of course, even if those arguments about "need" were true, any missiology which says that mission must necessarily flow "downwards" from gospel-rich to gospel-poor countries is a breeding ground for paternalism. Can we not accept that the majority world also has something to give in ministering to the West?

But all of these conversations about "need" and priority seek to order mission according to *our* priorities and values. We have already rejected the idea of a prioritization of "reachedness". Thankfully, there is a way to sidestep this statistical warfare, by moving from a conversation about human evaluation of Gospel priority to a conversation about the nature of God. *Mission which flows from the nature of God is done according to the character of God, and this provides a thoroughly different rationale for cross-cultural "going": we do not go across cultural and geographic boundaries because the statistics tell us there is a need to do so; we cross boundaries because this is the way God, in His divine character, chooses to order His mission.*

The cross-cultural mandate comes from the frequent Biblical motif that God deliberately commissions the foreigner and the outsider living incarnationally among a different people to be an agent of His blessing to the wider community: a fact to which the stories of Abraham, Joseph, Moses, Ruth, Daniel, Esther, and many others testify. In the New Testament, the examples of Peter and Cornelius, Phillip and the Ethiopian, and Lydia and those around her, also demonstrate God's desire to orchestrate the movement of people in order to bring the Gospel across cultures.

The rootlessness of the foreigner puts them in a place where they are a symbol of dependence upon God; the cultural difference of the foreigner puts them in a place where they naturally suggest a contrasting worldview and way of living to the people around them. At least historically the foreigner was in the position of guest and stranger, a position of relative social powerlessness - not, as in the majority of Western mission history, a position of relative social power - and it is surely significant that God's Kingdom is most clearly in evidence when it arrives by means of the guest perspective.

To put all of this simply, we do mission overseas because God delights in mixing it up. Looking at mission this way, in terms of God's deliberate action in creating cross-cultural people movements, also helps us to lift our eyes off the professional missionary and instead consider the many situations in which God is moving His people across the globe. This too is part of how God is going about His mission, and something we must pay attention to in our understanding of how mission will develop in the future.

Nevertheless, structures supporting mission need to be aware of this dual reality. On the one hand, there is a need to resource and empower churches whose understanding of mission is increasingly *primarily* local. As more and more contexts become increasingly multicultural, churches need to be prepared for the fact that local mission *is* cross-cultural mission, and that "reaching the unreached" - however we define it - can be done "from home"; and equally, support structures and organisations need to become more comfortable with this. Yet on the other hand, we also need to both encourage and support churches in rediscovering the centrifugal impulse of mission, and seeing a *geographical* sending in mission as something that proceeds from the heart of God Himself.

PROBLEMATIZING MISSION: AS TASK

We have already highlighted that we have implicitly conceptualized mission as a task. This is a deep-rooted and ubiquitous framing of the concept of mission. It can be seen in the Catholic encyclical *Ad Gentes*, which refers to mission variously as a "mandate" (s1), a "duty" (s5), and "task" (s6), as well as in Evangelical documents such as the Cape Town Commitment, which is firstly a commitment "to the *task* of bearing worldwide witness to Jesus Christ and all his teaching." (preamble)

In ecumenical circles, the WCC declaration "Together Towards Life" takes a markedly different note, referring to mission as the church's "response" (s55) to God's love, but it too affirms that "not only individuals but also the whole church together is called to evangelize" (s81), concluding that God has "given us the mission of proclaiming the good news to all humanity." (s101)

The problem, of course, with looking at mission in terms of a task is that

> [m]ission, relational in its nature in being derived from the God of love, becomes transactional. Add to this the focus on strategic planning, impact assessment by numbers, fundraising and it all becomes very difficult to retain dependence on the Spirit in any meaningful way.[10]

Another issue surrounding the conceptualization of mission as task is that it demonstrates clearly that despite a *notional* acceptance of the *missio Dei* approach (which we will examine in more detail later), our operational model of mission is still primarily human-centered. A truly God-focused missiology would accept that "mission is not primarily an activity of the church, but an attribute of God."[11]

---

10. Paul Bendor-Samuel, 2017. "Challenge and realignment in the Protestant cross-cultural mission movement". *Transformation*, 34(4):267–281.
11. Bosch, 390.

Within our organisation, we have established a culture of seeking the mind of God together as the primary means of decision-making, based on the principle that each member is indwelt by the Holy Spirit. When we are operating at our best, it is not logic or strategy that persuades, but a corporate sense of God's direction. We must be careful to retain this culture of dependence on Him as we seek new directions for mission today.

But speaking of mission as "task" does not just endanger our relationship with God; it also affects our relationship with those to whom we minister. They become the objects and we become the subject. We have already mentioned how there is a danger that language of "reaching", "unreached" and so on either subconsciously encourages us to see mission in primarily activist rather than relational terms, or is indeed perhaps a reflection of the fact that we are doing so. Either way, we need to be aware of both how our perception of mission and of the language which we use regarding it can have the effect of "othering" those we serve. Mission is clearly more than just a job to be done.

Is there another way in which we should learn to speak about mission rather than a task which we have to fulfil? Perhaps a way forward would be to speak of the church's *invitation* to join God on His mission.

For one thing, we can be sure that God's mission will continue with or without our involvement: an invitation may be turned down, but the party will go ahead anyway! This is the argument Paul uses in Romans 3:1-5: on the one hand, God's covenant purposes in making Israel a light to the nations do not depend on Israel responding "correctly". Their failure to be involved does not frustrate God's purposes. "God will be true to his original purpose both in creating man (1:18, 25) and in choosing Israel (2:8, 20), Israel's"falseness" notwithstanding."[12] On the other hand, however, there is much benefit to Israel in being part of God's covenant purposes - being entrusted with the very words and presence of God. So too with us. We are partners with God in His mission, but if we are not willing, His mission will continue - we will simply miss out on the reward of being close to Him and watching our Father at work.

For another, the language of invitation reminds us that we are the guests, not the host, and that the circumstances of our engagement may change at any time. When you are invited to follow someone, you go at their pace and follow their route, with all its twists and turns. Invitation to join God on His mission therefore carries with it elements of uncertainty and discovery; we have to be discovering and rediscovering where we fit in, what the Master is doing, and where He is going next.

We are not *given* a task, such that it is then ours to carry out as we please, for us to project-manage in the way that we most think efficient and reasonable. Instead, we must be constantly reading the landscape, seeking out where God is at work, and where we fit in. This seems to capture more of the spirit of what it means to be involved in a mission that is not ours, but His.

PROBLEMATIZING MISSION: AS COLONIAL

At the same time, the fundamental concept of "mission" itself has come under fire from commentators such as Stroope, for three reasons - first, as it forms an assumption of mis-

---

12. James Dunn, 1988. *Romans 1–8*, WBC 38A, Grand Rapids: Zondervan, 1988, 140.

sion as "sending" which is not necessarily borne out in the Scriptural text. (However, he does not advance any exegesis to back up this line of argument.) Second, Stroope argues that "mission" carries connotations of perpetrating a Western, colonial model; third, because despite (or perhaps because of) the efforts to nail down its meaning, "mission" remains definitionally fuzzy.

The variety of definitions of mission demonstrates that mission is not just "one thing". Stroope argues that the distinction between "mission" and "missions" (that is, the overarching task of the Church as commissioned by Jesus and its operational outworkings in particular locations), and the distinction between "the mission of God" and the "mission of the church" are similarly hard to draw. Because nobody can say what "mission" really is, Stroope suggests we throw the whole terminology away. His suggested replacement, the term "humble witness", certainly deals with the colonial baggage of missions. But it is not clear what practical difference such a change in terminology would actually make: how "humble witness" would look different to "mission" is not spelled out in his book.

To comprehensively engage Stroope would take another book, but perhaps it is better for our purposes to see his post-colonial critique of mission as representative of both a wider soul-searching in the Western mission community, and a reflection of the growing influence of the challenge to Western models brought about by the rise of majority world mission. It is estimated that since the year 2000, there are more majority world missionaries than Western missionaries; it is now appropriate to speak of mission as now being a non-Western enterprise.[13] These majority world missionaries and missiologists have brought both direct critique and quiet alternatives to the Western model.

In particular, we can contrast mission "from below" with mission "from above". Historically and stereotypically, missionaries have arrived in mission fields that are poorer, less developed, and more "needy" than their home countries. And naturally, they have wanted to help; and with all good will, set to bringing their resources and expertise to bear on the local situation. Some missionaries did this in conjunction with the local people, based on their needs and their agendas and using indigenous resources - but many others did not.

On the one hand, this has meant that mission has come with an unconscious sense of paternalism and superiority on the part of the missionary: we, the blessed "haves", are bringing the Gospel to the poor "have nots" - based, of course, on a Western understanding of cultural and developmental superiority. Missionary newsletters emphasise the poverty and need of the people in order to highlight the benefits brought by the missionaries and justify their presence. When mission is carried out from above, it tends to erase those to whom we minister, reducing them to objects to be pitied, rather than human beings with their own agency and capabilities, to be related to and partnered with. "The pagans' pitiable state became the dominant motive for mission, not the conviction that they were objects of the love of Christ."[14]

---

13. Patrick Johnstone, *The Future of the Global Church*, xxx
14. Bosch, D., 1991. *Transforming mission: Paradigm shifts in theology of mission*. Maryknoll, NY: Orbis, 290.

On the part of hearers, however, mission in this mode has meant that the Gospel becomes intrinsically linked with the social and developmental benefits brought by the missionaries - education, health care, and material resources. I am not merely referring to the problem of "rice Christians", who accept faith in exchange for the material benefits it brings, but the more general point that when Christianity is presented "from above", it becomes seen as an aspirational faith, one which is the key to a better life. Of course, the coming of the Kingdom of God amongst a people *should* lead to social and individual betterment. But the faith experience of the missionary "from above" and the local believer can be quite different: where Christianity is not a privileged religion, coming to faith may not result in social preferment but persecution, ostracism or impoverishment. Christianity from above has little to teach about sacrifice.

I have to admit that I find this critique of mission somewhat hard to engage with, because my personal experience in mission was so different. In Japan, I was living amongst people whose levels of health, education, wealth and standard of living were higher than my own; the only thing I had to offer them was the Gospel, with no gimmicks to accompany it or to make myself feel better about my work.

Perhaps, though, this served to blind me to my own privileges, because this experience still does not compare with mission from below, where majority world missionaries are ministering to those in a position of wealth and privilege very much "above" them, or working in dangerous and restrictive areas without the protection afforded by a Western passport. In this they are closer to the original apostles, who saw themselves not as the bearers of culture and prestige but as "aliens and strangers in the world" (1 Pet 2:11) and whose message about a condemned criminal from a quiet backwater of the Roman empire was not cloaked in cultural and economic superiority but was instead "a stumbling block to Jews and foolishness to Gentiles" (1 Co 1:23).

It is no exaggeration to say that mission from below is rapidly becoming the dominant model of mission in practice, if it is not already. Even though the global discourse surrounding mission still currently revolves around Western organisations and voices, this apparent influence is disproportionate compared to the sheer number of majority world missionaries quietly transforming the face of missions. We will find, however, that the support structures which were appropriate for the privileged West are not appropriate for this kind of mission from below, and we must be careful to avoid sending out David in Saul's armour:

> Existing missionary models among Evangelicals have not been able to overcome the distances and barriers created by the comparative affluence of missionaries and agencies. The frequent tendency of Western mission agencies to bypass their indigenous partners and to perpetuate their own "independence" is an indication of failure, and growing poverty exposes that failure. The missionary dynamism of churches in the South could well be stifled and misdirected by an imitation of the expensive Western models of missionary organization. The future demands more models of non-paternalistic, holistic missions. An incarnational approach modeled by Jesus and Paul is the key.[15]

---

15. Samuel Escobar, 2000, "The Global Scenario at the Turn of the Century", in W. D. Taylor (ed.), *Global Missiology for the 21st Century*, Grand Rapids, MI: Baker Academic, 44.

THE MISSIO DEI: A PARTIAL ANSWER, AND SOME NEW QUESTIONS

Where Stoope sees the lack of clarity in the definition of "mission" as a problem, it could alternatively be seen as a positive feature. The fact is that the distinction between "the mission of God" and the "mission of the church" *is* hard to draw, by design. The barrier between God's activity in mission and our own is porous and fluid, because Christ and his bride are united and have become one flesh, and what God has put together, no man may put asunder.

If we are to accept that God is involved in everything and that He Himself blurs the boundaries between His mission and ours, then our understanding of mission has similarly got to be pluriform. Even within the narrow scope of reaching the unreached, we must consider the full range of human involvement within the mission of God. On the one hand, this mitigates against the strategic "magic bullet" approach which assumes that there is one single best way to do mission.

The *missio dei* understanding of mission is welcome for the way that it has widened the church's understanding of mission. Indeed,

> There has been very wide, uncontested acceptance that mission is God's... it is not that God has a mission for his church but that God has a church for his mission.[16]

---

16. Paul Bendor-Samuel, 2017. "Challenge and realignment in the Protestant cross-cultural mission movement". *Transformation*, 34(4):267–281.

Engagement with the idea of *missio dei* also helps to de-
lineate the boundaries of our responsibility. "Humans can
never claim ultimate responsibility for the earth and those
who dwell on it, for only God is *ultimately* responsible. This
relativing power of the concept of God protects human responsibility from its idolatrous and destructive tendencies."[17]

We may believe on one level that mission belongs to God,
but often our praxis gives the impression that we actually believe it belongs to us. In reality, we have a tendency to think,
as the late great Keith Green would say, that each generation
of believers is given the responsibility for that generation
of souls. This leads us to cling on for too long in situations
where the Gospel would be better served if we left, and to
overexaggerate our own importance in bringing the Gospel to
individuals, cities, people groups or nations. We act as though
God's mission depends on us—and not just "us" in general as
the people of God, but in the particular provisional people,
teams and organisations at work in particular ministries. Even
though we acknowledge that God brought us into these situations at a particular time, we subconsciously believe that the
same God is either not capable of or not likely to send anyone
else. This in turn means that those leaving the mission field
often leave with a sense of guilt and failure, as few (if any)
will leave because their "task" was "accomplished".

Missio dei reminds us that what we do fits into a much,
much bigger picture. It tells us that mission depends ultimately on Him and is orchestrated by Him, that He was at
work drawing people to Himself before any missionary entered a field situation and will continue to be at work after

---

17. Thomas Thangaraj, *The Common Task*, 65.

they leave. Thomas Thangaraj argues that while we have a responsibility to the world, it is only a relative responsibility, subordinate to God's ultimate responsibility, and can only be exercised "in a mode of humility and prayer".[18] This is tremendously freeing.

But the *missio dei* approach is not without its problems. Thangaraj argues that the process of missiology should be an inclusive conversation, and beginning with the *missio dei* - which presupposes a huge amount of shared theological background about the nature of God, the church, the Trinity and so on - "already forecloses the discussion and defines the direction of the process in predetermined forms."[19] For him, this is unacceptable as it shuts out non-Christians from the discussion; but even amongst Christians the term *missio dei* is built on the scaffolding of a huge amount of doctrines, not all of which may be shared.

John Flett goes further, stating that the *missio dei* understanding of mission was a necessary way of "rebranding" mission to avoid its human (colonial) past by seeking a divine mandate for it. But he also argues that the traditional understanding of the *missio dei* proceeds from a faulty separation of God's act from His being. When we say that God is a "missionary God", are we talking about *who He is* or *what He does*? There are problems either way.

In one case, we believe that God reaches out to the world because He is a God who is fundamentally all about relationships. When we apply this understanding of God to the church's role in mission, we perhaps subconsciously, assume that relationships within the church come first and witness

18. ibid.
19. Thomas Thangaraj, *The Common Task*, 39.

proceeds from it. We also assume that the church has (like God) an existence of itself, separate from its mission into the world. "As God's act is a derivative overflow of who he is, so the church's missionary act is [a] second step alongside its eternal nature."[20]

In the other case, we prioritize God's actions in history as the ultimate way of understanding who He is. Hoekendijk describes mission as "God's all-encompassing sending-economy: sending His angels, prophets, word, Messiah, Son, Spirit, apostles, Church, etc."[21] This becomes overbroad, making *sending itself*, not any particular act of sending, characterize the mission of God. In a sense, everything became mission, and so nothing became mission: there was no "hook" on which to hang the Church's involvement in God's "sending-economy".

Flett's solution to this dilemma is to maintain the union between action and being; as we are drawn into union with Christ, we also become participants in his action. The "hook", in this case, is reconciliation, and in particular the act of God in reconciling the world to Himself. Unity of relationships characterises *both* the internal life of God *and* His activity within the world. He draws out several implications from this position. First, that the church must always be a community that is both "reconciled and reconciling." God reveals Himself to the world both through, and as an overflow of, His internal relationship, and so a church which is witnessing to God must itself be a community which reflects that reconciling nature of God, both in its own internal relationship and in its participation in God's reconciling the world to Himself. Indeed,

20. Flett, J, 2009, "*Missio Dei*: A Trinitarian Envisioning of a Non-Trinitarian Theme", *Missiology* 38:1, 5-18
21. Hoekendijk, J, 1966, "Notes on the Meaning of Mission(-ary)." In *Planning for Mission: Working Papers on the New Quest for Missionary Communities*. Thomas Wieser ed. New York: NY, US Conference for the WCC, 41.

for Flett, it is in reconciliatory witness to the world that the church is constituted. We are a missionary community because we are brought into being by the reconciling work of God.

Missionary activity must, therefore, both bring forth and spring from reconciliation. Christian communities must learn to see themselves as the fruit and outworking of God's mission, which spurs these reconciled communities on outwards to participate in His mission themselves. At the same time, communities which are dependent on reconciliation with God for their very existence must also be demonstrating reconciliation on the horizontal level, between humans. It is often said that serving together in mission brings unity between Christians; we can also say that, conversely, where missionary activity brings disunity, it cannot be said to be mission as carried out according to the mission of God.

A secondary implication of the union between mission as God's action and mission as God's being is that "participation in the missionary act is the true nature of Christian piety". If God is truly reconciling in His very nature, then those who worship Him will do so by sharing both in His reconciling work and nature. "Active participation in the missionary experience of the community is the concrete form a living fellowship with God takes here and now": not singing a song or attending a service. Mission *is* worship, because it is the means by which we are taken up in the life of God.

Accordingly, Flett concludes that every Christian is indeed a missionary, quoting Karl Barth that unless this is the case, "our communities cannot be missionary communities, and, in point of fact, cannot be truly Christian communities at all."[22] We will consider the consequences of this in the next chapter, as we seek to circumscribe what we mean by "a missionary".

At the same time, living in a Trinitarian understanding of the mission of God has implications for missionary "strategy". "Mission cannot be something the community possesses, for mission is not lived out by the community in isolation." It is a constant dialogue with God, a joining in His life and work, in which both He and His community invite the world into reconciliation.

To summarize, we now have a picture of what it means to live out the *missio dei* from Trinitarian perspective: Christian communities recognising themselves as being constituted by mission; seeing mission as the primary means by which every believer partakes in worship of God; understanding mission in terms of God's reconciling the world to Himself and our partnering with Him in inviting others into that reconciliation; and demonstrating their own reconciliation by acting in unity with one another.

CONCLUSIONS

The question of the nature and definition of mission is a live and contentious issue in missiology, and has been for many decades now. Rather than attempting to forge a new defintion, we have looked at some of the key discussions in an attempt to chart a new way forward; a new way for us to understand mission organisationally, that can set the parameters of our thinking as we investigate what an organisation to facilitate mission should look like today.

---

22. Barth, *Church Dogmatics*, III/4:579

First, we recognised that there is an emerging common understanding of mission that erases the distinctions between "local" and "global" mission. While it is welcome that this encourages all churches and Christian communities to seek for their own entry point into God's mission - and organisations serving the cause of God's mission should find ways to encourage and resource them - we equally need to reassert that mission *does* have a geographical outward direction. This is drawn not from arguments about need or "reachedness", but from our examination of the character and nature of God in deliberately using the foreigner as a blessing and a symbol to the people amongst whom he or she resides.

It has been common to speak about mission in terms of a task given by God to the Church - so common, and for so long, that the framing is almost unquestioned and unnoticed. We have seen two reasons why it makes sense to move away from this kind of conceptualization: first, because of the way it objectifies those we serve, and second, because it suggests that we can determine and order the "task" according to our human understanding. Instead, language such as "invitation" encourages us to remember that mission is God's and that we are joining Him in His activity.

Another criticism of the modern mission movement has been that it is based on colonial models and heritage. Mission has come under much needed critique from mission movements from the majority world, in particular in terms of the engagement of Western missionaries often from a paternalist perspective, in terms of the way that they have engaged in mission from a position of social or economic power and have associated mission with Western civilization, and in terms of the way that they have or have not worked in genuine

partnership with local believers. At the same time, we have
yet to see the emergence of new models for majority world
mission which are uniquely suited to their contexts.

The *missio dei* has been a widely accepted understanding
of mission, and yet there has been little genuine impact on
models of mission in practice. Understanding that mission is
indeed God's frees us from taking on responsibilities which
are not ours to take, and, although it can be criticized as
lacking clear definition and implications, there are models of
the *missio dei* such as John Flett's Trinitarian model that can
help us shape our understanding. What God is in Trinity,
and what He does, is the same: reconciling relationships. This
gives us clues as to what mission must look like in this mode,
and this is something which applies not just to professional
missionaries but to all Christians, wherever they may be.

CHAPTER THREE

Missionaries and Mission Structures

Questions of missiology have a tendency to remain rather abstract: the exact nature of the mission of God is of intense theological importance, and yet mission agencies and missionaries can operate with provisional, "folk" missiologies. Missionaries tend to be activists, driven by the urgency of mission, who know intuitively what needs doing, and are eager to get out and do it.[1] On the occasions where there *is* space for reflection and the acceptance of a need for a new missiological direction, this does not often translate to change in praxis.

The *missio dei* is an example of this: it is a concept which has been around for many decades, which is broadly accepted, and yet, as we have seen, has not often impacted practical missionary structures in a radical or deep level.[2]

What I want to do in this chapter is to begin to intentionally apply what we have concluded about mission at a theological level in the previous chapters to the next conceptual level down, that of missionary personnel and organisations which serve them, and see how these operational structures and assumptions may need to change based on our reflections so far.

---

1. Bosch, D., 1991. *Transforming mission: Paradigm shifts in theology of mission*. Maryknoll, NY: Orbis, 333.
2. A counterexample would be Kirk Franklin's *Towards Global Missional Leadership*, which investigates the application of the *missio dei* principle to issues of leadership within mission movements.

WHAT IS A MISSIONARY?

In two magisterial books, Chris Wright has demonstrated the connection between the *missio dei*, God's mission, and the mission of the church, which he calls "the mission of God's people".[3] The principle that mission belongs to God, coupled with the fact that God works in and through covenant relationships with His people, has led to a search for a corporate understanding of mission. But there still remain questions as to how this understanding is translated into practice.

For one thing, *who* is it that carries out the church's mission? Is this mission carried out by all members of the church equally, or is the outward-facing element of the church's mission delegated to a specific set of individuals within the church? Do *all* members of the church need to be concerned with *all* aspects of God's mission - evangelical, social justice, environmental and so on - or can believers "specialize"? Or are these questions themselves evidence of an overly-individualistic mindset, and the reality is that ours is a truly corporate call, carried out in practice by the church as a body?

The Western Protestant mission model, from the time of Carey onwards, has operated from the unquestioned assumption that a "missionary" is a distinct role, a particular professional and full-time calling for a particular individual. This call is seen as located within the individual, independent of their relationship with the church. The church's only responsibility is to respond to the calling placed on the individual, by recognising, developing and supporting it. Mission in this model therefore proceeds from the individual and from there places demands upon the church.

---

3.   Wright, 2017, *The Mission of God's People*.

Within this individualized understanding of missionary work, it has been accepted that some Christians are missionaries and some are not; indeed, that a tiny fraction of a percent of the world's Christian population are members of this elite, dedicated class. Andrew Walls reminds us that "full commitment to the cause of missions was in practice always an elite movement."[4] Thus we need to be careful when evaluating statistics about numbers of "missionaries" sent or received in different contexts: the number of missionaries sent from the Philippines, for example, is enormous - unless you only count full-time, professional mission agency members! Thinking in terms of the Western model of elite mission can cause us to ignore what Samuel Escobar calls the "missionaries from below".[5]

Even where the mission call has been *popularised* - Bendor-Samuel gives OM, YWAM and the short-term mission movement as examples[6] - this has only extended to popularise *access* to the elite. In other words, the message of the short-term movement was that all Christians *could* be involved in mission; it never really extended to the idea that all Christians *are* involved in mission. While in theory, we talk about the "mission of the church", the reality still seems to relate to specific individuals within the church.

The recent popularity of the "missional church", which developed out of the work of Lesslie Newbigin and the Gospel and Our Culture Network, has attempted to tip the balance back towards both a more corporate and a more universal understanding of mission. But this movement is essentially

4. Walls, 2017, *Crossing Cultural Frontiers: Studies in the History of World Christianity*. Maryknoll, NY: Orbis Books, 219-221.
5. Samuel Escobar, 2003, *A Time for Mission*, Leicester: IVP, 15-16.
6. Paul Bendor-Samuel, 2017. "Challenge and realignment in the Protestant cross-cultural mission movement". *Transformation*, 34(4):267–281.

Western and predominantly local; it has little to say about
global mission. The emphasis of the missional church movement is a post-Christendom reconfiguration of ecclesiology,
to recontextualize it to "Our Culture" - by which is meant
Western culture. We see this in the manifesto book *Missional
Church*, which was subtitled "A Vision for the Sending of the
Church *in North America*".

Advocates of the "special call" model trace their view-
point scripturally from Acts 13:2, where the Holy Spirit com-
mands the church to "set apart" Barnabas and Saul for a particular mission calling. These two were "called" (v2) and "sent
out" (v4) by the Holy Spirit, which led them accordingly to
be "separated" (v2) and "released" (v3) from the church. The
alternative to the "spiritual elite" understanding of missionary work - in other words, the view that *all* Christians are
essentially called to be missionaries - also finds scriptural justification, this time in the Great Commission of Mt 28:19. We
can see this from the Catholic Encyclical *Evangelii Gaudium*:

> In virtue of their baptism, all the members of the Peo-
> ple of God have become missionary disciples (cf. *Mt* 28:19).
> All the baptized, whatever their position in the Church
> or their level of instruction in the faith, are agents of
> evangelization, and it would be insufficient to envis-
> age a plan of evangelization to be carried out by pro-
> fessionals while the rest of the faithful would simply
> be passive recipients. The new evangelization calls
> for personal involvement on the part of each of the
> baptized. Every Christian is challenged, here and now,
> to be actively engaged in evangelization; indeed, any-
> one who has truly experienced God's saving love
> does not need much time or lengthy training to go

out and proclaim that love. Every Christian is a missionary to the extent that he or she has encountered the love of God in Christ Jesus: we no longer say that we are "disciples" and "missionaries", but rather that we are always "missionary disciples." (p120)

Yet another understanding is the idea of the missionary nature of the church itself; that the church has a corporate call to participate in the mission of God, a kind of "group project" to which every member contributes in different ways. To Western ears, the Acts 13 passage above may sound extremely individualistic - we see the Holy Spirit calling individuals, and separating them away from their church context for ministry - and this may give the impression of providing a mandate for mission as a para-church activity. But in Paul Momo Kisau's commentary on this passage[7], we see the situation being interpreted rather differently.

Kisau emphasises not the freedom of the individuals *from* the church, but rather the continuity of the church community. First, he notes the role of the church in recognising the prophetic call upon its members; next, the faithfulness of the church in being prepared to release gifted prophets and teachers for service elsewhere; then, the church's commissioning and sending them, as representatives who were "going on behalf of the whole community of believers"; and finally in how how the church continues to see them as remote members of the community: "This sending may simply mean that the two were released from their teaching positions so that they could take up their new roles as missionaries." Simlarly, commenting on Acts 6, Chris Wright sees the mission of the church as a corporate call with individualized outworkings: "while the

---

7.   Paul Mumo Kisau, "Acts", *Africa Bible Commentary*, 1349.

ministry of the Word continued to be the urgent priority for
the apostles, the 'ministry at tables' became the priority for
those appointed to that task as *their* ministry. However, we
can also see that such priorities were not mutually exclusive."[8]

All Christians, then, are part of a Church which is called
to mission. As we saw in our investigation of the *missio Dei*,
taking seriously the mission of God means having an expectation that each Christian is involved in mission; that mission
is the normal Christian life and indeed that Christians should
see involvement in mission as their act of worship; and that
this mission is expressed through inviting others into God's
reconciling presence.

If every Christian is a missionary, if involvement in mission is an expected part of the Christian life, then surely the
purpose of any mission organisation can only be to facilitate
the *total* involvement of the whole Church in mission.

This is not, however, what actually happened.

WHAT IS A MISSION AGENCY?

Once the Evangelical movement established the existence
of a certain (priestly?) cadre of dedicated missionaries, the
logical next step was to create structures to support and resource these Christians. In 1792, William Carey called for the
establishment of a para-church missionary society to send
and support missionaries to the unreached. His proposed structures - a society which determines the strategies and fields to
be reached; committees to handle finance, missionary selection and what we now call member care ("to provide them
with necessaries for their undertakings"); and financial support raised by Christians in the sending country - have essen-

---

8.   Wright, 2017, *The Mission of God's People*, 215.

tially set the model for world mission agencies over the past two hundred years.

Not everyone would be a missionary, but as a second best, everyone could be involved in the mission of the church through supporting those who were. In the same way that an individualistic reading sees Paul and Barnabas as "separated" and "released" from their local expression of church, the Western cross-cultural mission movement constructed itself as having an independent organisational existence, operating alongside (but distinctly outside) the local church.

The voluntary society was established on the basis of a special call for the few, and therefore from its inception it took on a sort of centripetal focus: the society existed to serve the needs of its members and only its members, and where it reached out into the wider church, it was only either to gather more resources from the church for itself, or to promote itself to the church with the aim of acquiring more members. The traditional Evangelical mission agency, then, did not faciliate, resource or equip the missionary activity of others outside its own organisational boundaries; or where it did, it would do so with the expectation that those others would come to join in or work through the organisation. When we look at the balance sheet between resources given and resources received, it would be fair to say that the mission society did *not* support mission; it only supported itself.

This competition for the church's resources naturally brought the mission agency, as a para-church organisation, into tension with the churches, at least in the West. Ralph Winter introduced us to the concepts of "modality" and "sodality" in order to argue that the distinction between church and agency was both a necessary and biblical one; but his article can be seen as a *post hoc* rationalisation of the Carey model. Winter gives only pragmatic reasons that, essentially, the church cannot be trusted to get around to it, but there is no intrinsic reason why mission needs to be done through a separate body to the local church. Indeed, alternatives to the modality/sodality dichotomy are clearly possible, as we shall see later.

It is in response to some of these tensions, as well as to changes in global and church contexts, that have led the structures and aims of the mission agency to evolve over the past two hundred years.

THE CAREY MODEL IN A CHANGING WORLD

One reason for the Carey model was, essentially, cultural. Within the culture of nineteenth century Western capitalism, if someone wanted to achieve a goal that they could not do as an individual, the usual way to approach the problem was to form a society, appoint a committee, and take up subscriptions. That was the structure used in the culture of the time to organise a group of people to do more than one person could do alone - the social equivalent of the joint stock corporation.

Many things have changed in the culture since then which may make the traditional model less relevant. For one thing, sending a person to live in a different country is no longer a "hard thing" requiring the co-ordinated effort of many people; it can be done as an individual, without the support of a voluntary society. In the nineteenth century, it was a major undertaking to migrate to a different country and start life there; but in our generation, missionaries also benefit from a culture of mass migration and people movement. The overseas worker is no longer exceptional.

The second thing which has changed is the nature of co-operation and organisation, particularly in Western cultures. With the rise of the "network society" in the 21st century,[9] the way that we do achieve "hard things" and in particular the structures of co-operation that we use to pursue social change, have changed. The network society no longer trusts the delegation of its interests to monolithic entities or external organisations, preferring to work through temporary networks of grass-roots activism. *Organisations* have given way to *movements*. What characterises the movement, as I am using the term, is that it is not formally constituted as a corporate body, but draws its power from networks of relationships.

To take a recent political example, the American gun lobby, the National Rifle Association - a clear case of a centrally-organised voluntary society - is facing the greatest challenge to its power from Never Again, a loose association of student activists. They have no organising body or formal structure, they hold no meetings, have no positional leaders (although they certainly have functional leaders), and collect no subscriptions or dues. Extinction Rebellion would be another example of a distributed social activism movement. Social media is used to co-ordinate their activities; the network itself is the organisation.

In other words, the movement is not *externalized* as an separate association or organisational entity. It has no reality distinct from those people who subscribe to its aims; it is comprised purely of the people. Its boundaries are fuzzy, rather than binary. One is a supporter and participant, not a member. As Brian Knell puts it,

---

9. Castells, M., 2000. *The Rise of the Network Society*, Cambridge: Blackwell.

[T]tere is a suspicion of organisations today. People like to work in teams, where structures and rules are based on relationships. Mentoring is popular, again because the personal relationship is predominant. Organisations on the other hand are seen as large, impersonal, mysterious, uncontrollable, unwieldy institutions that cannot be influenced from outside. One consequence of this is that people today are very reluctant to join anything and if they do it is for a limited time with a particular objective in view. Membership, particularly long-term membership, is becoming out of fashion.[10]

What does this mean for our mission structures? In one sense, the problems of the relationship between churches and mission agencies go away if there is no external "agency" there.

When the task of mission is vested in an external body, a mission society or agency, it is too easy for mission to become someone else's responsibility. This is more apparent when we look at the missional church movement, another expression of the same cultural change. The concept of "missional church" has attempted to de-externalize the church and reconceptualize it as its people, rather than some independent entity with its own existence. If there is this thing "out there" called "the church", then as an individual my relationship with it is that of subject and object; the church is "it" and not "us". But when the church is conceptualised as the people, not the building, the clergy, or institution, then it is natural to understand the work of the church to be the responsibility of each believer,

---

10. Knell, B., 2003, *From societies through agencies to consultancies - a trend in mission organisations*. "Survive or Thrive? Is there a future for the mission agency?" conference, Global Connections.

rather than something that I pay my tithe for someone else to do.

To what degree have we made the mission agency "it" and not "us"? Have we constituted the agency as an external entity which takes upon itself the responsibility for participation in God's mission and by doing so removes the impetus for church members to find their role and involvement? In a networked society, it may be necessary to kill the mission agency as we know it if we are aiming for total involvement of the church in mission. Concepts of joining (and hence being subordinate to) an external organisation may need rethinking in favour of participating in a common mission movement.

However, it is important to remember that not all the world is a networked society. In some parts of the world, trust in institutions and central organisation is still strong. As we will see later, in parts of the world which are rapidly developing as mission sending contexts, there is a felt need for more formal organisational support of mission. We cannot apply the networked model without contextualization. It is a product of its time and culture, just as the voluntary society was a product of its time and culture.

Outside of the West, however, mission structures still look very much like the Carey model. Despite the significant growth of mission and missionary activity from the majority world, we have yet to see the emergence of a genuine alternative model of missionary organisation. On the whole, majority world missions have, either consciously or by default, organised themselves structurally along similar lines to Western agencies. For example, WEC's partner agency in Nigeria, CAPRO, was established by Nigerians but deliberately adopted the WEC principles and practice as its constitution.[11]

---

11. Tesilimi Aderemi Lawanson, "Calvary Ministries (CAPRO): A Case Study of a Model of

Where there are differences between the operating assumptions of Western and majority world agencies, they are generally at level of emphasis, values, and praxis, rather than a fundamental re-imagining of the mission agency concept. Robin Thomson writes that South Asian missions movements are of the "more relational family type" compared to Western corporate organisational structures; people and resources flow back and forth between diaspora churches and home communities, both through formal structures such as charities and through informal networks, and "the style is family based and entrepreneurial."[12] According to Heung Chan Kim,[13] one major difference in values is that majority world missions are characterized by a close relationship between the missionary and their sending church. The value of partnership is also seen in the praxis of AsiaCMS, which we will investigate in chapter eight, which aims to always "co-send" missionaries in partnership with local sending entities.

Structures for the future of mission, therefore, may need to look different to *both* the voluntary society and to the de-externalised network.

THE CHANGING NATURE OF MISSION AGENCIES

Knell further traces a trajectory of change in the language around mission agencies: the 18th century "voluntary society" of Carey evolved into the faith-based "mission society", where missionaries felt a life-long "call" not merely to involvement

Majority World Initiatives in Christian Mission", in Wan and Pocock, eds., *Missions from the Majority World*, Pasadena, CA: William Carey Library, 346.

12. Robin Thomson, 2010, "Asian Mission Movements from South Asian Contexts", in Tan, Ingleby and Cozens, eds., *Understanding Asian Mission Movements*, Gloucester: Wide Margin Books.

13. Kim Heung Chan, "A Newer Missions Paradigm and the Growth of Missions from the Majority World", in Wan and Pocock, eds., *Missions from the Majority World*, Pasadena, CA: William Carey Library, 11.

in mission but to the principles of the organisation, which saw itself in familial rather than functional terms. That is, you joined an agency to work with a certain kind of person, not to do a certain job. (To some degree, WEC is a "mission society" in this mould.)

In the 1990s and 2000s, the focus moved from "mission society" to the "mission agency", with a task orientation and a short-term focus. Emphasis on a life-long call for the select few was replaced by an acknowledgement that any Christian could be "used" in mission according to their gifts, so long as there is a need for them within the work of the agency - and when that work is done, so too is their involvement with the agency. Mission was open to anyone, but those involved still had a special call to a dedicated role, at least for a time, before returning to "secular" life.

Knell argues that the next generation of organisations will see themselves as "world consultancies", specializing in a particular segment of the mission experience and offering their services at cost to the mission community as a whole:

> If, for example, a church wants to send someone to black Africa, they might well buy the services of one group to provide orientation, another for health care, and others for finance management, theological training and language learning. They may even choose a further group or indigenous church with which to be linked for direction and member care in Africa. We are blessed in the UK with agencies who can provide all the range of services that a church sending someone overseas will need, but it is because churches have thought that they have had to plug into one uncontrollable system for all these services

that many have decided to be completely independent and have thereby deprived themselves of the
experience available. I do believe that churches and
individuals would be willing to pay for services that
they believe are important, well-presented and good
value for money.

We can detect this trend already emerging: missionary preparation has already been outsourced from organisation-inter-
nal training programmes to mission colleges and training centres; Stewardship provides financial services; specialist missionary health care and even member care consultancies (such
as the Well in Chiang Mai) have been available for a number
of years. An important question within this study is therefore: if all of the "outsourcable" functions of a mission agency
are outsourced, what is left? *What is at the core of a mission
organisation?*

In combination with the network society issue mentioned
above, it makes sense to ask if we even need mission agencies
at all.

WHAT SUPPORT IS NEEDED?

The trend in the development of agencies also parallels
the trend we have seen in re-conceptualizing mission as primarily the responsibility of the local church. The move from
agency to consultancy, in particular, assumes a more confident and assertive local sending body (church, denomination,
etc.), together with increased capacity caused by the growing
normalization of cross-cultural travel, life and work.

In other words, when cross-continental travel, communication, international banking, and so on were not widely
accessible, local churches were almost *forced* to send their

missionaries to a specialist entity. Now these things have become easier, mission has become essentially democratized and the cost of entry has been drastically lowered. Churches, who perhaps were always somewhat uneasy with the presence of the mission agency and who are now increasingly assertive in their identity as the legitimate vehicle of mission, are now more able to play their part without the need for an intermediary. Knell's "consultancy" model assumes the future of mission agencies to be playing a support role to these local sending structures - an ideal which resonates strongly with the ideas of mission that we have investigated so far.

In this context, it might seem tempting to do away with the mission agency altogether, to see it as an outdated and no longer necessary vestige of a pre-globalized age. Indeed, this is an idea which has raised its head a number of times in missions history. For example, the Scandinavian Pentecostal missions of the early 20th century deliberately disbanded in favour of congregational models of mission, based on the theological convictions of Lewi Pethrus in Sweden and Thomas Ball Barratt in Norway that the local church was the *only* legitimate bearer of mission.

The experiment did not last long; fifteen years after the missions were closed down, it was found that "[n]o one had a general overview of the situation, and a need for administrative assistance and cooperation was felt. Thus the fear of a central organization that would affect the independence of the congregations, a fear that was still existent in many quarters, was surmounted by acute need."[14] Little by little,

---

14. Mikaelsson, L., 2018. "The Norwegian Pentecostal Foreign Mission: A Survey of Mission History with an Emphasis on Organization, Expansion, and Gender", in *Charismatic Christianity in Finland, Norway, and Sweden: Case Studies in Historical and Contemporary Developments*, Cham: Springer International Publishing, 49–77.

the system reasserted itself: Gunnerius Tollefsen became the mission secretary for the Kristiana church in Oslo, but was available as a point of contact and support for all congregations across Norway. Regional and national mission field conferences were re-established, and soon accepted by the national Pentecostal conference. Within 3 years, the mission agencies were back again. The value of inter-missionary support and co-ordination simply proved to be too high to go without.

This is particularly true as we look at mission beyond the West today. Just because local sending entities have increased *access* to cross-cultural mission, this does not mean that they have the confidence and institutional experience claimed by Western churches. In their global survey of mobilization, Mantega and Gold found that while more experienced sending countries were looking to streamline the mission organisation, removing bureaucracy and support structures in favour of a more lightweight operation, this was not seen in newer sending countries, whose missionaries long to see *greater* development of organisational structures:

> The lack of props, or support mechanisms, was mentioned frequently enough by voices from new sending nations that it earned a place here amongst mission organisation retardants. Interestingly, if respondents from traditional sending contexts complained about anything, it was too much infrastructure. Here, respondents from new sending contexts lament the lack of it.[15]

---

15. Mantega and Gold, 2016, *Mission in Motion*, Pasadena, CA: William Carey Library, 203.

In particular, respondents mentioned the need for candidate development and screening, training, member care, mobilization (and specifically the presentation of opportunities for missionary service), and accountability. While in theory each of these things can be carried out effectively by the local church of denomination, it is these areas which have been reported as lacking and being in need of development. Reflecting on "challenges facing Asian Missions", Kang San Tan also wrote that one challenge is "inadequate sending structures (candidate screening, missionary preparation, field leadership, member care). In particular, member care is still lacking when compared to the level of care provided by International Missions."[16]

So we have seen that while we believe that on the one hand, the church is essentially missionary, and that the invitation to God's mission is one which involves every Christian, we also find that the support structures provided by the mission agency cannot easily be done away with.

But equally this does not imply that the mission agency needs to *take over* from the churches, which is what ended up happening in the Carey model. In contrast to the voluntary society which brought members from the church into itself and then autonomously organised them into a mission movement, can instead we envisage structures of mission mobilization and support which seek to develop the capacity of local churches and church structures as they facilitate their members in finding their place in God's mission? We will present a potential example of this kind of structure in chapter eight.

---

16. Kang San Tan, 2010, "Who is in the Driver's Seat", in Tan, Ingleby and Cozens, eds., *Understanding Asian Mission Movements*, Gloucester: Wide Margin Books.

AGENCIES WHICH EXIST FOR OTHERS

As mentioned in chapter one, we are going about this search for future models of mission from a position of a commitment to church planting. One way in which a church planting perspective can help us in our search is that it gives us a set of principles, a worldview, by which we can evaluate and critique the missions movement. Church planters - at their best - strive for reproducibility, multiplication, and missional impact. How does the Western missionary model look from a church planter's eye?

I have described how the Carey model was predicated on the idea of an elite missionary force, and then developed organisational structures to support such a force. In the language of the missional church, the Western mission agency model was, paradoxically, not missional; rather, it was attractional.

For one thing, no priority was given to replication *of the mission agency*. While we hope to make disciples who make disciples, and plant churches which plant churches, no such replication principle was applied to the mission agency itself; new workers were absorbed into the monolith, rather than spun out to their own organisation. Granted, the foreign agency had enough work to be getting on with without the additional effort of trying to replicate itself. But from a church planter's perspective, building a movement of replicating mission agencies, adapted to their individual context, is a more sustainable approach. Ralph Winter claimed that the biggest failure of missionaries in the past 200 years is not church planting, but mission planting.[17] In a somewhat cynical sense,

---

17. Winter, R. D., 1978, "Ghana: Preparation for Marriage", *International Review of Mission*, 67(267):339-340.

our failure to plant missions is ultimately helpful, as it has allowed new sending contexts to experiment with their own structures rather than inheriting and replicating our Western structures wholesale and without contextualization; but the failure of vision in not prioritizing the planting of new movements bears much reflection.

Missionary recruitment consisted of extracting people from their (church) context and re-situating them in a different context, that of the mission agency, which would then be the primary source for their feeding and nurturing, as well as their ministry. As with evangelism, recruitment by extraction creates a gap between the original context and the new context, and restricts the flow of influence in both directions.

More significantly, extraction evangelism (and by extension, extraction recruitment) is often likened to fishing with a line rather than fishing with a net - it requires significant investment and resources in a few individuals at the expense of engaging the many. If we are attempting to extend the definition of "missionary" to include all Christians rather than an elite cadre, then the nature of what it means to support missionaries, and the organisational and relational structures to enable such support, will also need to radically change. For one thing, organisations will need to become more missional, more outward focused, seeing themselves not as *responsible* for mission but as *enablers* of it. Our para-church mission structures will need to see themselves, as Knell argues, as service providers to facilitate the mission of others.

As an example, one organisation which has shifted from "doing mission" to providing consultancy services to resource the mission of others is SIL. To a certain degree, SIL was always involved in providing linguistic and training services to the Bible translation community, but over the years, it has developed more of a focus on supporting and resourcing the work of others, in particular through a renewed focus on development of and partnership with local translation projects. Indeed, while the popular image of SIL within churches will still revolve around Bible translation, in reality it is becoming more and more difficult to find SIL members who are directly involved in Bible translation themselves!

In 1975, John Bendor-Samuel proposed that SIL develop a more flexible approach to membership, arguing for the inclusion of national workers and national organisations. At the same time, SIL was responding to both internal and external critiques of the impact of its work, which also pointed to the need to partner with national churches and develop their capacity both in terms of scripture engagement and local language preservation and development. The immediate problem with these partnership efforts was the question of how they should be funded.

One response was the formation of the Seed Company, a fundraising entity desgined specifically to financially resource local translation projects. However, questions have since been raised as to the effectiveness of external fundraising for remote projects; despite the due diligence of fundraising entities, it is hard to avoid favouring projects based on the quality of their application for funds, which may or may not have any bearing on the quality of their execution. Other parts of SIL have since attempted to grapple with the question of funding and principles of self-sufficiency as applied to local partner projects.

In 1999, Wycliffe International (now Wycliffe Global Alliance) and SIL adopted Vision 2025, the goal of seeing a Bible translation for "every people group that needs it." This forced SIL to work in new ways to accelerate global Bible translation, and brought a renewed focus on partnership, collaboratively with churches, mission organisations, and local translation groups.

> One of the important indirect impacts for SIL was the rapid growth in demand for technical services and consulting help generated by the rapid start of many new language programs. When SIL was the primary initiator of new language programs the growth in the capacity to provide technical support remained close to the demand for it. Since Vision 2025, there has been much faster demand for these services than growth in capacity to provide them.[18]

In other words, SIL's activity became driven in part by the needs of external programs, and the need to provide linguistic services to the projects of others, more than by the programs that it initiated. It became an agency which sought primarily to service the needs of others than its own.

What is interesting about this change is that it came about as a deliberate choice after considerable reflect on SIL's global impact. Whereas previously a value for the organisation had been its capacity to produce, in particular to produce new translations, a shift towards thinking in terms of impact allowed it to focus on facilitating and developing the work of others. In essence, the question shifted from "How do *we* achieve this?" to "How do we *see this achieved?*"

The cultural change within the organisation was not necessarily easy, and the transformation towards being a service organisation is still continuing. Still, this shift "from produc-

---

18. SIL International, *Remembering Our Journey*.

tion to impact" and the resulting changes in priority as the organisation has sought more intentionally to multiply its efforts through partnership and consultancy, is a significant example of a missiology developed out of the trends we have been discussing.

So what can the SIL example teach us? How can a church planting organisation learn from this transition, and what would it mean to be a service provider in this kind of ministry practice? To begin with, who would such a service provider provide services to?

The audience for a church planting service provider would naturally include, at the broadest level, any mission-minded Christian who are wanting to be resourced, mentored or guided in church planting; our goal is that all Christians accept the invitation to journey with God in mission. But as we have noted, the locus of missional involvement is shifting from the individual to the church. There are many mission-minded churches both in the West and in the majority world which are wanting a greater involvement in world mission but which wish to retain more control over the process than they would traditional have by "handing over" their missionaries to a mission agency.

SIL's moving from production to impact allowed it to partner with and resource other translation projects. In the same way, a church planting agency which saw itself as a facilitator and enabler of mission would be free to provide services to other mission agencies and sending organisations, as well as to existing church planting networks seeking to reach out into new areas. An impact focus leads to a generosity of spirit, resourcing and facilitating others to enable *their* goals.

A church planting mission which shifts towards this kind of focus would need to find new ways of describing its impact, as counting teams, churches planted, or people coming to faith, is more difficult when these things are achieved by partners over whom one does not have direct influence. New definitions of success will be needed, and new goals to celebrate. But the humility required to see oneself as playing an indirect part in the broader picture of God's mission is both more realistic in the context of a complex world and more theologically satisfying than counting individual successes and achievements.

WHERE TO FROM HERE?

In a sense we have now reached the end of part one of our investigation. I have aimed to bring some theological and missiological perspectives on the question of what a church planting mission should look like, in part through critique of existing models and by reflection on missiological thought in the light of our current context.

We have seen how the inherited model of the mission agency places a high priority on the individual, by seeking to empower and support a small number of "called" elite Christians. Recent corrective measures within agencies have sought to take the church and the corporate dynamic of mission more seriously, but these can be seen as reactions to help *maintain* the status quo, rather than fundamental changes to it. The agency is not longer parallel to the church, but neither is it overlapping.

However, we have also seen that even though commissioning cross-cultural workers in the 21st century is considerably easier than doing so in the 19th, cross-cultural mission requires support, and that these support structures are sufficiently indispensable that where they are removed, they are quickly recreated in another form.

So while there is still a need for something like a mission agency, there is no longer a need for it to be both mother and father of mission - and indeed to attempt to be so would demonstrate a failure to take seriously the sovereignty of God in mission. Instead, we can seek to empower the church in mission by moving towards a model which supports, facilitates and enables the mission of others, and which seeks impact over achievement in church planting.

But what, practically, should that look like? What is it that we want to spend our time supporting, facilitating and empowering, and how should we do it? To answer that, we must spend some time looking at the world situation and the possibilities that it affords.

CHAPTER FOUR

The world has changed

As we plot a new course for mission structures, it is important to remember that the existing structures with which we are familiar are products of their time and context. As such, it makes sense to consider in what ways the world of today differs from the world of a hundred or two hundred years ago when the Western model of the mission society was established.

In this chapter, rather than comparing the two worlds directly, I will look at a number of the most pressing global trends of today. These trends will help us to consider the ways in which existing models of mission will require adaptation to fit with present and future situations.

THE CLIMATE EMERGENCY

The most pressing global need at the moment is the fact that "our house is on fire." While for many years, climatologists have warned that anthropogenic climate change has set in motion major changes to the planet's habitability, these concerns have often seemed abstract, technical, long-term and ultimately invisible. But over the past few years, these invisible changes have become increasingly more visible in terms of their human consequences. Climate changes are no longer the concern merely of scientists, but impact upon migration policy, food and resource availability.

As an example, the city of Cape Town relies on winter rainfalls to replenish its water supply. However, the poleward migration of moisture corridors and changes to the jetstream meant that Cape Town suffered three consecutive years of dry winters,[1] leading to sustained drought, and by 2018, the city came within weeks of turning off municipal water supplies. The causes of the water shortage in the city were not *simply* climatological - population growth, waste, city planning failures and political instability all combined to exacerbate the situation. But this is merely a reminder that climate change can interact with existing structural weaknesses and dramatically magnify their effect.

These concrete effects of climate change are now regularly included in global strategic intelligence reports and contigency planning. For example, the US Director of National Intelligence released a briefing reporting hypothetically on a future scenario from 2028:

> Changing climate conditions challenged the capacity of many governments to cope, especially in the Middle East and Africa, where extended droughts reduced food and water supplies and high temperatures suppressed the ability of people to work outdoors. Large numbers of displaced persons from the region often found they had no place to go as a series of dramatic terrorist attacks in Western countries drove those governments to adopt stringent security policies that restricted immigration.[2]

1. Pedro Sousa et al, 2018, "The 'Day Zero' Cape Town drought and the poleward migration of moisture corridors". *Environmental Research Letters* 13:12.
2. Director of National Intelligence, 2017, "Near Future: Tensions are Rising", *Global Trends*.

How will these effects impact upon mission? It is hard to predict the full scope of the impact, but we can be certain about a number of areas.

First, there is the phenomenon of "climate refugees", or more strictly, people displaced in the context of natural disasters and climate change. Most people in this category are internally displaced (and hence are not technically called "refugees"). For example, agricultural economists in the US are already modelling migration flows from Florida, Louisiana, and the mid-West to Western states.[3] Studies such as theirs show how climate-related migration will have an economic impact, restructuring local economies.

However, there are increasingly situations where those fleeing the effects of climate change are forced to do so across borders, and these true climate refugees are often placed into situations of conflict or violence. This mix of climate change and conflict is known as "nexus dynamics", and demonstrates again that climate change exacerbates existing global insecurities. I will discuss the impact of forced migration on mission in more detail later in this chapter.

As the climate changes, conflict over water supplies and farmable land will intensify. There is considerable debate on both sides as to how strongly the 2006-2007 Fertile Crescent drought was linked with the Syrian war (in particular as it did *not* lead to conflict in surrounding countries). Direct correlation is hard to prove, as are single-cause explanations. There is also some debate as to the extent to which the climate change / conflict discourse is the result of colonialist

---

3. Qin Fan et al, 2018, "Climate Change, Migration, and Regional Economic Impacts in the United States", *Journal of the Association of Environmental and Resource Economists*, 5:3.

attitudes.[4] However, there is a consensus amongst researchers that intensifying climate change will lead to increased conflict in the future.[5] This instability will make circumstances more difficult for cross-cultural workers, and potentially reduce access to the Gospel in the most remote and rural areas, but at the same time may drive migration into urban areas.

What about direct impacts upon mission? As Global South countries are now both a significant part of the global mission movement and also most likely to be impacted by the effects of climate change, it makes sense for them to be "ground zero" in the interaction between climate change and mission. In 2018, I visited a missionary training facility in Brazil, which was founded 30 years ago in an area of farmable land next to a river. Today the river has dried up and the college relies on a system of tanks for its water supply. In the future we can expect changes to Global South (and ultimately Global North) missions caused by further non-viability of mission facilities such as headquarters buildings and training centres. Missionaries relying on agriculture for financial support - either themselves or from their home countries - will need to be consider the viability of their support over the long term.

Finally, and particularly in the Global North, a greater environmental awareness is already causing changes to attitudes towards short-term international travel. The short-term mission trip, seen as a key motivating factor for recruiting career missionaries into long-term service, is now being evaluated in terms of its environmental impact.[6] As mentioned

---

4. Cullen Hendrix, 2018, "The Sophomore Curse: Sampling Bias and the Future of Climate-Conflict Research", *New Security Beat* blog
5. Katharine J. Mach et al, 2019, "Climate as a risk factor for armed conflict." *Nature* 571:7764.
6. Premier Christian News, 2019, "Young people call for flight-free mission trips." https://www.premier.org.uk/News/UK/Young-people-call-for-flight-free-mission-trips

in chapter two, the most authentic experience of mission is that of cross-cultural life from the guest perspective, and so exposing people to this kind of mission is still an important part of mobilization. At the same time, a more globally nomadic youth culture can be expected to have greater experience of "life overseas" without a specific short-term mission programme. Mobilizers will need to hold these two aspects in tension and potentially come up with new approaches. Instead of creating distinct "mission trip" experiences, it would make more sense to develop training and resources to encourage those living and working overseas to think of those visits as missional opportunities.

POST-SECULARISM, POST-LIBERALISM, POST-CHRISTIANITY

The US National Intelligence Council publishes regular strategic assessments of global trends. In its most recent report, the main threats to international security are described as coming from increasing political populism, isolationism, and authoritarianism leading to a post-liberal world order. A retreat to nationalism and unilateralism means that "debates over moral boundaries — to whom is owed what — will become more pronounced, while divergence in values and interests among states will threaten international security." At the same time, this populism is being driven by increasing popular opposition to the negative aspects of globalization, coupled with rising economic inequality. "The combination of these events led to a more defensive, segmented world as anxious states sought to metaphorically and physically 'wall' themselves off from external challenges, becoming 'islands' in a sea of volatility. International cooperation on global issues, such as terrorism, failing states, migration, and climate change eroded, forcing more isolated countries to fend for themselves."[7]

While especially evident in Europe and the US, this post-liberal tendency is not merely a Western phenomenon. Indian nationalism is being married to religious conservativism in an increasingly official policy of Hinduisation. Authoritarian and illiberal "strongman" rule is visible in Hungary and Turkey, but also in Brazil and the Philippines.

In many cases, post-liberalism has combined with post-secularism, and religious conservativism has been co-opted to serve and validate these illiberal impulses. We need to evaluate these developments carefully. What are the implications for mission? In the past, Christians were sceptical of the secularisation hypothesis and welcomed the development of post-secularism, but did not anticipate the rise of toxic religion allied to illiberal state governments. A post-secular turn may *theoretically* increase popular openness to religion, but what kind of religion is generated as a result? The establishment of either *de facto* or *de jure* state religions - such as in the cases of India - and even state Christianity - such as in Hungary and Russia - mean that the situation is more difficult for other religions. We can expect to see greater persecution of Christians and decreasing access to missionaries in these countries, both officially in terms of visa restrictions and unofficially in terms of mistrust and lack of responsiveness.

We must also consider the impact of the co-option of religion by the state in cases where that religion is Evangelical Christianity itself: Brazil, the US and the Philippines are examples of where conservative Evangelical churches and the

---

7.   Director of National Intelligence, 2017, "Near Future: Tensions are Rising", *Global Trends*.

state have entered into a symbiotic, and in some cases, complicit relationship. This impacts upon mission in two directions. First, both the local and the global reputation of evangelicalism is harmed by its involvement with illberal authoritarian politics which have little in common with the Gospel of Jesus. As Christianity Today magazine describes the situation in the US:

> [T]he alliance of American evangelicalism with this presidency has wrought enormous damage to Christian witness. It has alienated many of our children and grandchildren. It has harmed African American, Hispanic American, and Asian American brothers and sisters. And it has undercut the efforts of countless missionaries who labor in the far fields of the Lord. While the Trump administration may be well regarded in some countries, in many more the perception of wholesale evangelical support for the administration has made toxic the reputation of the Bride of Christ.[8]

Evangelical Christianity's association with political conservativism can easily become a millstone for the missionary - particularly one from such an evangelical culture - to carry as part of their gospel witness.

In an another direction, however, there is a danger that through this complicity, the culture of these evangelical churches becomes remade more and more in the political image of their state sponsors - as isolationist, nativist and nationalistic politics become established as cultural boundary markers for evangelical leaders and their congregations, do we really expect to see a growing care for the poor and for the foreigner?

---

8. Timothy Dalrymple, 2019 "The Flag and the Whirlwind", *Christianity Today*, December 22.

How will this impact on both the quantity and the quality
of missionary sending from these areas? It is hard to see
the combination of these two things - a damaged reputation
of evangelicalism, particularly amongst younger people, and
reduced concern for the problems of the outside world - as
producing a healthy missionary force. *It is perhaps therefore
more appropriate to focus missionary recruitment, training and
development, on areas of the world which have not made Con-
stantinian bargains with the state.*

Jonathan Ingleby points out that populism itself is a multi-
faceted concept. "It may be possible, if we break down populism into its parts, that the church (and therefore ultimately
mission) may be able to ally itself to some aspects of populism." In a sense, the Protestant mission model is a populist
one, in that it stresses the empowerment of the laity in opposition to elitism and clericalism. "Even nationalism is not
necessarily an enemy... In South Korea the identification of
the church with the national resistance to the Japanese occu-
pation, led to remarkable Christian growth."

Evangelical Christianity has generally thought of itself as
living beyond politics - neither allied to right, nor to the left,
but only to the kingdom of God. The movement's assumption
of its own neutrality often blinds it to its actual, more nu-
anced (and generally politically conservative) position. At any
rate, an attitude of studied neutrality and political disengage-
ment is no longer sustainable in a post-liberal world which is
deliberately seeking to co-opt religion. Ingleby tells the story
of an English missionary to South Africa in the apartheid
days, who said to his black African congregation on arrival
that he did not want to talk about politics: 'Oh,' relied the
people, 'but we do!' Missionaries going to the Middle East,

for example, will need to be able to speak intelligently about their home government's position on Israel and Palestine - studied neutrality in such situations will often be interpreted as indifference to, or worse, approval of human suffering. *Missionary education and preparation will need to take into account these factors, aiming to develop more politically astute and self-aware missionaries.*

In Europe, we are seeing the development of a post-Christian culture, meaning that the church no longer has, or is quickly losing, its influence on society. The number of people identifying as Christian has fallen from a half in 2008 to a third in 2018, and "religious decline in Britain is generational; people tend to be less religious than their parents, and on average their children are even less religious than they are". The British Social Attitudes survey directly highlights the difficulty of transmission of the faith: whereas a child of two non-religious parents is extremely likely to grow up non-religious (with only 6% of the population becoming religious in adulthood), a child of two religious parents only has a 50% chance of maintaining their religious identity. The upshot of this failure in transmission is that while one third of Brits aged 75 or over are members of the Church of England, amongst 18-24 year olds, the figure is 1%. Younger generations in the UK have little or no knowledge of the Bible or Christianity, and an increasing number are being brought up with no religious faith, to the extent that we can consider British youth to be essentially unreached.[9]

---

9. Figures from Curtice *et al*, eds, 2019, *British Social Attitudes 36*. See also Murray, 2004, *Post-Christendom: Church and Mission in a Strange New World*, Carlisle: Paternoster Press.

The situation is similar across other parts of Western Europe. According to Operation World, France, the Czech Republic, and Spain now have a population of one percent or fewer evangelical Christians. As well as considering this European trend in our missionary strategy, we must also prepare for the possibility of similar reversion in other countries where Christianity is current fervent but marked with generational change: South Korea and the US are showing signs of similar demographic decline amongst the Christian population, and if this appears to be a trend within a particular generational expression of global evangelicalism, we must also be on the look-out for similar issues occurring in current Evangelical boom areas such as Latin America, Nigeria, Uganda, and parts of East Asia.

Rather than a pure focus on individual evangelism, churches will require greater support in assisting families with the transmission of the faith and building a Christian identity.

MIGRATION AND REFUGEE SEEKERS

As we have seen, the climate emergency has lead to increased numbers of displaced people, for both direct reasons (climate refugees, who are unable to continue to live in a location due to the changing climate) and for indirect reasons (refugees caused by, for example, conflicts generated by a scarcity of food, farmable land, water or other resources). Indeed, mass migration, particularly of refugees, has been a defining global trend of the 21st century so far, and this is expected to continue to increase; the trends of postliberalism and state-sponsored persecution that we have just been discussing will only add to the problem.

While the proportion of people living outside of their countries of origin has remained relatively stable at 3% of global population over the past 100 years, world population growth means that the absolute numbers of migrants are at their highest ever. In particular, the number of people classified as "persons of concern" by the UNHCR - forced migrants such as refugees, asylum seekers and internally displaced people - has risen dramatically in the past 30 years, from 14.58 million (0.3% of global population) at the end of 1988 to 74.79 million (1% of global population) at the end of 2018.

As I have mentioned in chapter two, the foreigner living in a foreign land has a special place in the mission of God. On the one hand, living away from family support networks and the security of shared language and culture places one in a situation of weakness and dependence; on the other, it gives a set of new opportunities, new experiences, and thereby new choices. The migrant experience - particularly for the first generation of forced migrants - comes with a "critical distance" from the culture they have fled, and thereby provides the openness and freedom to selectively integrate these new dimensions into one's life.

With these trends in mind, those involved in sending missionaries can no longer assume that the most "natural" place to reach people of a particular people group is within their country of origin. Most Western agencies are still unconsciously structured around the idea that a people group is located in a particular nation; this is no longer an appropriate assumption. Someone wishing to reach Somalis might be best placed not in Somalia, but in Ethiopia, Germany or Egypt. Of course, when asylum claims and other immigration procedures are in play, some people will be motivated to convert to Christianity as a way of bolstering their case for remaining in the country: Iranians in the United Kingdom are currently turning to Christ in large numbers, and while many are converting for genuine reasons, others have more mixed motives. But very few people come to Christ for totally pure reasons: wanting to feel closer to a community of friends, gratitude for love and care received, and material benefits are often involved in a decision. From a discipleship perspective, the motive for conversion is less important than long-term fruitful growth. But where there is genuine commitment to discipleship, a migrant population may be a *more* effective place to minister than a home population.

As well as first-generation forced migrants, there are increasing numbers of settled communities and diaspora groups around the world. (We will only consider the question here of mission *to* non-Christian diaspora communities. In the next chapters, we will investigate mission "through" and "beyond" diaspora communities - that is, the missional nature of Christian diaspora communities.) In many cases, these settled communities are religiously and culturally conservative, sometimes more than in their home context as they seek to maintain group cohesion as a minority.

But even so, there may be good reasons for considering missionary outreach to settled diaspora communities. Despite the issues of openness and receptivity, a diaspora group's host country may be more accessible and less restrictive for a missionary than in their country of origin; for example, someone wishing to minister to Somalis may be better positioned to reach out to Somali diaspora communities in Kenya than than in Somalia itself.

More generally, high migration rates and the existence of diverse diaspora communities challenge the structural assumptions of sending organisations. Country-based "field" structures which assume an equivalence between people group and nation need to be challenged. A Spain-based team may look at the people God has brought around them, and deliberately choose to focus on Romanians, not ethnic Spaniards. A team wanted to reach out to Turks might decide to situate themselves in Germany or the United States. Agency structures need to be flexible enough to coordinate *both* fellowship between teams working in a given location *and* teams working cross-nationally to reach particular people groups. Neighbours Worldwide in the UK is an example of a structure which relates teams across a geographical area working amongst different people groups, but this can also be coupled by a greater sharing of information, resources, and prayer between teams focused on the same people group around the world.

Additionally, mission thinking historically divided the world into reached and unreached *areas* rather than reached and unreached peoples: Europe and North America are reached, Asia and the Middle East is not, Africa and South America are somewhere in the middle. The reality at present is that the world is much more of a mosaic, with pockets of Christianity within non-Christian communities, and pockets of unreached people living alongside Christian communities. This means that for missionaries attempting to reach the unreached, there are almost always local resources available. If we are thinking in terms of impact rather than production, it is much more beneficial to spend time mobilizing, training, supporting and resourcing local Christian communities to become involved in cross-cultural ministry.

This applies both to "reached" and "unreached" mission fields. In "unreached" areas, settled diaspora Christian communities are more permanent and viable over the long term than the often transient mission team. For example, mobilizing Brazilian diaspora churches in Japan or Mexican churches in Spain to reach their hosts is more sustainable and reproducible than attempting to plant churches oneself. But at the same time, those seeking to reach Bangaladeshis in the United States may want to mobilize local churches of other ethnicities because of the shared sense of the migrant experience.

URBANISATION AND TRANSCULTURALISM

The world we live in has rapidly become more urban. Whereas in 1950, around 30% of the world's population lived in cities, by 2018, 55% of the world's population were urban, and this is projected to rise to 68% by 2050.[10] Older mission organisations with a focus on the unreached such as our own have historically seen the unreached as located in hard-to-reach rural areas, but this is no longer true; although no direct figures are available, I estimate that around a third of the world's unreached people live in cities.[11]

---

10. United Nations Department of Economic and Social Affairs, 2018, *World Urbanization Prospects*.
11. If we were to assume that unreached peoples are distributed evenly throughout the countries they live in, and hence that their urbanization rates were equal to the national urbanization rates, we would arrive at a total of 2.1 billion urban unreached out of 4.3 billion total unreached. (48% urban) However, this assumption is obviously overoptimistic; one reason that groups are unreached is because of remoteness and lack of access to the Gospel. So the question becomes one of approximating an appropriate discounting factor to bring down the 48% figure to a more reasonable amount. But looking at the first billion unreached people, most people groups are based on *national* rather than specifically ethnic or tribal identity, allowing the assumption of normalized distribution, and so the discounting factor is not as high as one might imagine.

One impact of city dwelling is the phenomenon of transculturalism, often described as a global youth culture, although its effect is not strictly limited to the youth. While global cities have always been places where cultures meet (*multicultural* environments), *transculturalism* refers to an environment where cultures blend to form a new hybrid culture. This tendency is increasingly the case at present for two reasons: first because increased travel and migration means that they are in themselves becoming more culturally diverse, but also because cities are connected to each other through information and media networks. As we are all watching the same TV programs and viral videos, listening to the same songs, visiting the same websites, and consuming the same products, this can lead to erosion of local cultural values, and replacement by universal, often liberal, values.

According to Soquier, transculturalism makes mission more accessible for both short-term and long-term missionaries, as they have a higher level of shared cultural and linguistic overlap. A young missionary from Kerala may well have more in common culturally with a young person in Cairo than with an older person in their home state, and will therefore require less cultural adaptation and training. Soquier gives the example of Paris, where French millenial slang includes elements of English, Arabic, and terms borrowed from African languages, while English-speaking artists and celebrities are promoted. This is "not an excuse to bypass language learning, but a release from the angst of language in preparation for mission work".[12]

12. Benajmin Soquier, 2016, *Missions in Global Cities*, unpublished essay, available at https://www.academia.edu/37676475/Missions_In_Global_Cities_How_Can_The_Gospel_Message_Move_Beyond_Postmodernism_In_Order_T

Further, transcultural millenials are more culturally fluid, able to "put on" and "take off" cultural identities with considerable ease,[13] a phenomenon known as "transpatriatism".[14] While on the one hand there are considerable benefits to recruit traditional, full-time missionaries from and to global cities, this phenomenon of transpatriatism reminds us of a new need in mission. We now have a generation which is increasingly living and working cross-culturally, and regarding this as normal and unremarkable; this generation should be challenged to see themselves as missionaries in their daily lives, and support structures should be put in place to resource and equip them. As mentioned above in the section on the climate emergency, it may become necessary to reimagine the "short-term mission trip" by identifying young expatriate workers, and training, resourcing and mentoring them to develop a missionary worldview.

The fact that younger global citizens are increasingly used to and increasingly expecting to work across national and cultural boundaries also asks some important questions about the practice of many mission agencies, including our own, of organising recruitment, orientation, and short-term mission on national lines. International mission agencies as multinational and multicultural communities are intrinsically attractive to a more globally-aware generation. While personal and local contact is still important as part of mobilization and recruitment, there would be a positive benefit to coupling this with *orientation and short-term programmes organised along regional or lines*. As well as celebrating and

13. Richard Slimbach, 2005, "The Transcultural Journey", *Frontiers: The Interdisciplinary Journal of Study Abroad*, 11:205-230.
14. Paul Scheffer and Liz Waters, 2011, *Immigrant Nations*, Cambridge, UK: Polity, 211.

highlighting the agency's multicultural nature, this may also increase efficiency gains through streamlined administration and the avoidance of repetition.

Finally, within the global city, one can find significant gatherings of Christians from many different countries and significant gatherings of non-Christians from many different countries. Each of these cities - Manila, Cairo, Hanoi, Lagos, and many others like them - is not merely its own mission field, but is actually its own miniature world. Within this "world", diverse multicultural teams can be mobilized to reach a diversity of people groups, both monocultural and mosaic. It would therefore make sense to facilitate networks between diaspora churches within these global cities so that they can build their own local "missions movement" to serve the "world" inside their cities.

THE AGING POPULATION

In general, the world is getting older; life expectancy is increasing and population pyramids are shifting more towards working-age and older people. This is already evident in Europe and countries like Japan, but will become a global trend. Mission to and by the older generation will need to be factored into current strategies.

To take the example of Europe, the old-age dependency ratio (the ratio of people aged 65 and above to those aged 15 to 64) in the EU was 12% in 1950 (8 working age people to every person 65+), rose to 29.9% (3:1) in 1950, and is projected to increase by 21.6 percentage points to 51.2% in 2070. This has been caused by a number of factors including increasing health, leading to life expectancy growing from around 65 in 1960 to 81 today, but has also led to decreasing birth rates across Europe.

What are the implications for the church and what are
the missiological implications? In Eastern Europe it is common for families to take responsibility for care of the elderly; this will become more common in Western Europe too.
Where there are elderly people without family, the church
will need to take on this responsibility, so we envisage a
need for Christian care and mission initiatives among elderly
Europeans. We see examples of this kind of ministry in the
Pilgrim's Friend Society in the UK as well as the King's Gar-
den nursing home centers in Japan.

Loneliness, isolation and feelings of uselessness are far
greater amongst the elderly, especially in Eastern Europe.⊠
There will also be the need and opportunity for mission for
connecting people across generations, making neighbourhoods
aware of their elderly people, and bringing seniors together
to fight loneliness and uselessness.⊠ Contextualizations of the
Gospel which speak to God's work in creating community
and "putting the lonely in families" will be appropriate responses to the spiritual needs of seniors.

Traditional churches and denominations have a high percentage of elderly people, and so will experience rapid decline
as the generations shift. This will have financial implications
for missionary support, as well as the viability of traditional
congregations.

However, longer life and greater health brings the potential for retired people to become "second career" missionaries; financially independent, mature Christians can be a great
asset, particularly in parts of the world where age and experience is respected a source of wisdom. Challenging older
Christians to a cross-cultural missionary life post-retirement
is already common in places such as Korea, and within my

own agency we have a number of second-career missionaries from a number of countries. But it is not yet a mainstream part of mobilization and recruitment policies.

Finally, the global demographic shift towards an aging population raises a number of important questions for field missionaries. First, to what extent do they see older people around them as a distinct people group to be reached? At least in the West and often in Africa, evangelism and mission has tended to focus on youth, partially due to the perception of increased receptivity of children and teenagers, but perhaps more to the point, as part of a wider cultural erasure of older people. Honouring and respecting the elder members of society by seeing them as legitimate recipients of God's love and mercy is itself a way to demonstrate Christian values.

Second, how does the Gospel overcome this cultural erasure through the building of genuine communities? While recognising the distinct needs of older people, there is also a need to integrate them into cross-generational communities. In some parts of the world, the church is one of the few arenas where young and old mix. This again is an opportunity for missionaries to demonstrate the distinct values of the Kingdom of God, but it is one which requires intentionality and determination.

Finally, mission teams will need to be intentional about explicitly mobilizing second-career missionaries, which will include thinking through the implications of working in cross-generational teams - navigating any additional support needs that they may have and any team pressures that this will imply.

CONCLUSIONS

Perhaps a key word which would describe the world situation we find ourselves in today is "fluidity": fluidity of movement of people, fluidity of culture, fluidity of situations affected by environmental, political and demographic pressures. When our vision of the world is largely static, it is easy to establish categories and strategies in a command-and-control manner. But as we begin to see the world of today as fluid, mission structures will need to adapt a similar fluidity in response.

In particular, the increasing movement of people has created a mosaic world, with global cities as microcosms of the world in themselves. On the one hand, this challenges simple distinctions and definitions within our mission structures - the distinction between sender and receiver, the association between people and place, the distinction between reached and unreached - but on the other, a mosaic world provides opportunities for networking and partnership at multiple levels. There is therefore an urgent need to reconfigure our structures to take advantage of these opportunities.

2

The Road Ahead

CHAPTER FIVE

Eight ways forward for the world mission movement

One of our key findings so far is that the world is a complex place which defies binary divisions and simple explanations. Accordingly, it would not make sense to offer one simple prescription for the future of mission - a kind of magic bullet, one-size-fits-all solution. Nor would it be possible to make such a prescription in a top-down, command-and-control manner. The world is a mosaic, and so is the mission world - it is a diverse and polyconcentric community of communities, and each of the many groupings which make up the mission world has its own values, specialisms, priorities and practical approaches. This is how it should be.

In this context, it seems more appropriate to consider a diversity of suggestions, a number of ideas to be experimented with, each of which are potential and partial responses to the situation we find ourselves in. They will vary in terms of their scope, complexity, and the impact and disruption they will have on existing mission structures. Some of these suggestions will be explored in this chapter, whereas others will briefly outlined and developed further in the following chapters.

ESTABLISH NETWORKS OF MISSION CATALYSTS

The single most important transformation for a mission organisation of the future is to become catalysts of grassroots and church-based mission. Mission catalysts do not seek to recruit missionaries to an organisation but instead mobilize and mentor both individual missionaries and mission-minded churches through their mission journey.

In addition, they assist missionaries (whether full-time, bivocational or migrant Christian workers) to access training, funding, financial management and structural services; encourage them to network with other local and like-minded workers, including those from other mission organisations; and catalyse the formation of *ad hoc* teams. Meanwhile, they train and equip sending churches to retain the responsibility for member care and support.

Doing this will encourage the growth of new mission movements as well as providing means for non-traditional missionaries to be supported and encouraged in their ministry. This idea will be more fully explored in chapter eight.

TECHNOLOGY AND COORDINATION

The past two hundred years have seen an explosive degree of technological advancement, particularly the greater communication opportunities provided by the Internet and pervasive mobile phone connectivity. While the mission movement has attempted to make use of these advances, technological innovations in mission have not been evenly distributed, with most technological development (with significant exceptions) still originating in the West and often producing material representing a Western perspective. Additionally, many resources and platforms replicate a Western individualistic model of evangelism and discipleship, and do not contribute to the holistic creation of a Christian community, whether off-line or on-line.

Such "Internet evangelism" and "Internet discipleship" could be improved and facilitated by ensuring true collaboration between technological innovators and Christian workers with on-the-ground experience of language, culture and worldview.

More generally, this speaks to the need for supporting those wishing to support the world mission movement using specialist skills and gifts, and providing them with not just the resources and training required to think missiologically and theologically about their technological development, but also with the expertise and insight of workers on the ground. These aspects will be examined in chapter six.

NEW STRATEGIC APPROACHES

Two centuries ago, there were major areas of the world where there was absolutely no history of Gospel witness; the priority was propagation. For better or worse, the main missionary strategy was to take existing models of Christianity to parts of the world where Jesus had never been named and to replicate them there.

In today's mosaic world, however, there are few contexts which are truly virgin territory into which the Gospel can simply be poured. Church planting now takes place in areas where there is generally a history of Christian mission already, in contexts of other religious faiths, and often where mission has been attempted but "has not been very successful"[1].

---

1. David Bosch, 1991. *Transforming mission: Paradigm shifts in theology of mission*. Maryknoll, NY: Orbis, 477.

Because of this, the focus must shift from simply "trying harder" at propagation, to active development of new missionary approaches. These new approaches will needed to be guided by the context, the available resources, the personality and gifts of the team involved, but principally by the Spirit of God - and so it is unwise to prescribe what such new approaches might look like. The following ideas - neither of which are truly new, but equally neither of which have been deployed at scale - are representative examples of new approaches which may merit further investigation.

NON-RESIDENTIAL MISSIONARY

In 1987 the Foreign Mission Board of the Southern Baptist Convention commissioned its first Non-Residential Missionary, as part of a new project to expand missionary activity into closed countries. Bruce Carlton's DTh thesis[2] charts the development of the non-residential missionary role into its present-day counterpart, the Strategy Coordinator.

The SBC's non-residential missionary concept combined two different ideas. The first was that the missionary, expecting to have to leave the country at short notice at any point, should not seek to establish a ministry of their own but to catalyse, train and mentor others. The second was that the missionary in a closed country would enter with a separate "visa identity" - business person, student, tourist, etc. - rather than in an overt missionary role, which the SBC had insisted on up to that point. Over time, this second idea became more important as the idea of sending workers into closed countries under another guise gained acceptance within the

---

2.   Bruce Carlton, 2021. *Strategy Coordinator: Changing the Course of Southern Baptist Missions*. Oxford: Regnum.

mission, and hence eventually the name became misleading, as half the members of the NRM programme *were* actually residential in their countries. The issue became one of identity - it was not that they were non-residential; it was that they were not residential *as missionaries.*

At the same time, the NRM idea was mainstreamed throughout the organisation, even in countries where missionaries *were* able to be resident and with a missionary identity. This further ensured that the initial, catalytical aspect of being non-residential was sidelined. The "Church Planting Movement" approach, which attempted to revisit some of these more catalytical ideas, should be viewed with this background in mind - that missionaries should be *prepared* to minister without being resident, but that in practice they generally would be.

But genuinely pursuing a non-residential strategy - that is, working purely in a mentoring and support role to local Christians for short periods in person and remotely over the longer term, while intentially not developing a permanent ministry of one's own - would seem to be a worthwhile idea to experiment with. Such a genuinely mobile approach to church planting echoes the practices of Paul and the early apostles in their missionary journeys: although it is accepted that Paul spent as much time as possible physically present in the initial stages of a church plant; while the compressed timeline of the book of Acts means that

> one may get the impression that Paul was, almost exclusively, an itinerant preacher. This is not correct, particularly in view of the fact that in some places he

stayed for longer periods (about one and a half years in Corinth, two to three years in Ephesus).

However, it is true that

he thinks regionally, not ethnically; he chooses cities that have a representative character. In each of these he lays the foundations for a Christian community, clearly in the hope that, from these strategic centers, the gospel will be carried into the surrounding countryside and towns... Furthermore, Paul is founding local churches, which he seeks to nurture *through occasional pastoral visits and lengthy letters, and by sending his fellow-workers to them.* [3]

Such a strategy has built-in protections against dependency on the missionary team and more generally on outside resources, and encourages Christians even at an early stage of church growth to make use of their own gifts in dependency on the Holy Spirit.

NEAR-NEIGHBOUR EVANGELISM

Another change from the missionary praxis of the past is that the idea that "unreached" means "remote" is no longer true. In fact, 57% of the world's unreached people live within 300 miles of another people group which has a significant Evangelical population. [4]

---

3. David Bosch, 1991. *Transforming mission: Paradigm shifts in theology of mission.* Maryknoll, NY: Orbis, 130, emphasis mine.
4. I'm defining "significant Evangelical population" somewhat arbitrarily as having more than a population of more than 100,000 Evangelicals according to the Joshua Project database.

Half of these *boundary peoples* can be found in Asia (particularly South Asia). There are also significant numbers of boundary people groups to be found in West Africa and the east coast of Africa. Current mission workers can evaluate the needs of local Christians and, where necessary, be involved in supporting and resourcing them to reach out to their neighbours. We should not automatically assume that these local Christian communities *lack* any mission vision for their neighbours and need external input to awaken such a vision. They may well have, and they may already be successfully engaging those around them. The world mission movement can, however, humbly and prayerfully offer partnership and support where it is required and requested.

When considering a near-neighbour strategy, we must also be aware of the lessons of history. Robert Blincoe[5] has written persuasively about the failure of the "Great Experiment" to reach the Kurds by a similar process of attempting to "reform" the nearby Nestorian churches and implant within them a missions vision for the Kurdish people.

Blincoe highlights a number of reasons why the strategy failed. In the first place, denominational differences between the missionaries and the local churches led to resistance and suspicion. The end result was that local Christians who did accept the missionaries' teaching separated and formed their own denominations. Granted, there was a considerable doctrinal gap between the Nestorians and the Protestant missionaries which would not necessarily be the case when Evangelicals are working with other Evangelicals. Even so, the position of an outside missionary attempting to bring a change

5. Robert Blincoe, 1998. *Ethnic Realities and the Church: Lessons from Kurdistan*. Pasadena, CA: The Presbyterian Center for Mission Studies, pp. 23–39.

in vision and practice to an existing church is exceptionally delicate.

Secondly, missionary effort was directed primarily towards Christians. Although Kurdish evangelism was the end goal, it became an indirect goal, and was effectively displaced by the direct goal of teaching and preaching within churches. Finally, the missionaries landed in the middle of a political struggle between people groups, bringing their resources and power to one particular (Christian) people group and thereby appearing to favour one group over the group they were ostensibly there to reach.

What do we learn from this story? Firstly missionaries who come *uninvited* seeking to "support" and "inspire" other churches in a particular direction must reckon with their own "teacher complex", and seriously consider the appropriateness of their mission as well as the risks that it carries. Second, though, even those who come to churches with a clear invitation to support their outreach to another people group must do so in full awareness of the ecclesiastical and political situation they are entering. Finally, near-neighbour ministry cannot be done as a proxy for one's own mission but as part of a genuine partnership of love, commitment and involvement, an expression of the missional unity of the whole church across borders - that is, not as missionaries as party A using Christians as party B to reach the unreached as party C, but as different aspects of the Church working together in God's mission.

As with the non-resident missionary concept above, supporting and encouraging the evangelistic activity of others through partnership is itself a legitimate form of mission, and one which should be encouraged as a possible alternative to primary involvement.

NEW FINANCIAL MODELS

We have looked at the impact of the global South missions movement, changing global attitudes towards missionaries in terms of visas and access to countries, and the rise of a culturally nomadic youth generation. We have also considered the need to engage the whole church in mission, with the consequence that not all missionaries will follow the classic pattern of being fully funded by donations from overseas; if this is done, then the dividing line between "missionary" and "non-missionary" will begin to blur. The need to mobilize and support those who would not traditionally be regarded as "full-time missionaries" will run alongside the need to allow for bivocational and non-traditional income models in those specifically sent by churches and mission agencies.

Some of these non-traditional income models will be explored in chapter seven.

DIASPORA MINISTRY IN A MOSAIC WORLD

Mission agencies initially operated on the basis of essentialist understandings of ethnicity and nation-state - the Vietnamese are in Vietnam and the Egyptians are in Egypt - and, although this has developed somewhat over the intervening years, vestiges of this understanding remain in the structural and organisational assumptions of today's mission agencies. Mission fields and branches are *generally* country-specific, and even where they are organisation around an transnational ethnic group rather than a country (for example, the Kurds), this is still bounded by physical location. Diaspora ministry, where it is present at all, is usually placed "off to the side" as an exception to the standard model.

But as we have examined in chapter four, the world is increasingly mosaic in nature, with significant populations of people outside of ethnic "homelands". Diaspora ministry is no longer an optional extra, but must be integrated fully into an agency's operations.

Diaspora ministry has many dimensions. The Lausanne Diaspora Leadership Team[6] proposes a four-way typology of diaspora ministry: the first is ministry *to* the diaspora, in terms of directly evangelising non-Christian overseas. The next stage is ministry *through* diaspora, which means diaspora evangelizing other members of same diaspora people group. There is also ministry *across* diaspora, referring to diaspora evangelizing other diaspora communities. Finally, there is ministry *beyond* diaspora, which means diaspora evangelizing the indigenous community. To this, from a mission perspective, we can also add ministry *from* diaspora, by which I mean mobilizing diaspora members for mission overseas, including in their country of origin. All of these elements need to be considered in a diaspora ministry strategy.

The first two elements are well known, and many organisations have been involved in ministry to the diaspora as an intentional missional strategy for many years. In terms of mission to the diaspora, it is well known that there is often a greater spiritual openness amongst a people who are outside of their traditional home country. For example,

> only 2% of the Taiwanese population is Christian; yet 25-30% of Taiwanese immigrants in the US are Christian and as many as two-thirds of the members of Taiwanese Christian congregations are converts.[7]

---

6. Lausanne Committee for World Evangelisation, 2010, *Scattered to Gather: Embracing the Global Trend of Diaspora*, Manila, Philippines: LifeChange Publishing.
7. Jehu Hanciles, 2008, *Beyond Christendom: Globalization, African Migration and the Transformation of the West*, Maryknoll, NY: Orbis, 296.

Similar trends have been noted amongst overseas Japanese[8] and Iranians, although in other situations, particularly where there is a "settled community" of second generation migrants, there can often be the opposite effect, whereby religious and cultural conservatism is a boundary marker to establish and maintain group cohesion. Mission agencies and evangelists operating along a "people group" strategy must consider these tendencies when situating teams for evangelism, and equally, teams already present in a country or locality should be aware of the needs of diaspora communities where they are situated.

Diaspora churches have themselves been involved in outreach through the diaspora. "Immigrant Christians and their descendants have a striking record when it comes to winning converts among immigrants."[9]

The further three elements are less well developed. Many African churches in the UK, for example, are attempting to move into mission beyond diaspora, but have only seen significant success in mission through or across diaspora. More mobilization and support could be provided to encourage diaspora churches to reach out beyond and from their communities.

MINORITY TO MAJORITY MISSION

Another approach worth pursuing is mission *beyond* diaspora, the use of large evangelical populations who are an ethnic minority in an area to evangelise the majority people group. As Lesslie Newbigin reminds us, "the first witnesses to

---

8. The Japan Christian Fellowship Network estimates that Japanese are "70% more open to the Gospel when they are overseas", although it is not clear how this is measured.

9. Jehu Hanciles, 2008, *Beyond Christendom: Globalization, African Migration and the Transformation of the West*, Maryknoll, NY: Orbis, 379.

the gospel in Antioch were not missionaries but refugees."[10] God's hospitality calls us to move beyond binary notions of culturally dominant groups as hosts and migrant and minority peoples as guests. Instead, in God's hospitality, God is host and we are all invited by the Spirit to participate with humility and mutuality in God's mission.[11]

According to the United Nations migration statistics for 2019, there are currently an estimated 270 million people living as migrants (defined as being "someone who changes his or her country of usual residence, irrespective of the reason for migration or legal status"). Of those, I estimate that around 16 million are Evangelical Christians.[12] Many of these are in areas where the surrounding population is largely non-Christian.

Identifying and supporting with these churches in their mission and outreach opportunities, if it can be done in a true spirit of partnership, can be a fruitful alternative to direct engagement in mission amongst a people group, and the partnership itself can be a witness to the unity of the Gospel across cultures.

MOBILIZING DIASPORA MISSIONARIES

Moving to the concepts of mission *across* and *from* diaspora, for Hanciles, "every Christian migrant is a potential missionary".[13] Indeed, the ability of diaspora congregations to

---

10. Lesslie Newbigin, 1982, "Cross-Currents in Ecumenical and Evangelical Understandings of Mission", *International Bulletin of Missionary Research*, 6:4, 146-151.
11. Jooseop Keum (ed), 2013, *Together Towards Life*, Geneva: WCC Publications, 71.
12. Based on the nationalities of those involved (from UN migration data) and the prevalence of Evangelical Christianity in their home countries (from Joshua Project data), adjusted slightly to recognise the fact that in many countries it will be specifically the Christians who are persecuted to the point of becoming asylum seekers.
13. Jehu Hanciles, 2008, *Beyond Christendom: Globalization, African Migration and the Transformation of the West*, Maryknoll, NY: Orbis, 378.

reach other diaspora groups of unreached people is a genuine source of excitement:

> These congregations represent a cutting edge of Christian growth in America. They are Christianizing groups whom American missionary agencies expend enormous amounts of resources and effort to reach in distant lands, often with modest results.[14]

How should mission agencies respond to this? In one sense, there is an argument for just letting them get on with it! Perhaps one reason for the effectiveness of these congregations is that they share the diaspora experience with those they are trying to reach, and so external involvement (particularly from the "host" culture) would in fact make them less effective.

But at the same time, this may be an idealised picture. There are many diaspora churches which - like many indigenous churches - are more concerning with maintaining and discipling their own people, and do not see themselves as a missionary people. If majority world missionaries, also themselves living the migrant experience, can unlock these congregations of "potential missionaries", can also resource and support them in their needs, then this "cutting edge" of Christian growth can become considerably sharper.

We should also not underestimate the potential for mobilizing and recruiting from migrant congregations to serve as overseas missionaries, either through returning to their own countries or going to a third country. Examples such as the Monglian overseas worker's churches in Korea demonstrate the fruitfulness of missionary recruitment from the di-

---

14. Jehu Hanciles, 2008, *Beyond Christendom: Globalization, African Migration and the Transformation of the West*, Maryknoll, NY: Orbis, 297-298.

aspora.[15] Deliberate attempts should be made to see diaspora churches as part of an integrated mobilization strategy.

SERVING DIASPORA CHURCHES

Existing mission agencies are right to be excited by the opportunities afforded by vibrant, growing diaspora churches. But they must see them as more than just opportunities for *them*, and more as opportunities for the Kingdom. Indeed, traditional agencies may need to rethink some of their assumptions and attitudes towards the diaspora churches. While preparing this section, I was asked how we can engage diaspora churches for mission and integrate them into our work.

Such questions assume that new churches need "engaging" so that then we can "include them in our teams." The suggestion is that they have no mission vision at the moment, and when we have imparted a mission vision to them, we can put them to work for *our* purposes. They do not know what to do, and we know what they should do. These questions reflect attitudes that we may hold subconsciously about mission. African diaspora churches in particular, who are critically evaluating the colonial legacy of Western missionary activity, will be very sensitive to these attitudes.

The truth is that many diaspora churches do have a missions vision for Europe; they are part of denominations in their home country which send missionaries to Europe; they network and partner with mission agencies and other churches in order to bring about this mission vision. While some of them lack the resources and expertise to reach Europeans for Christ, we cannot assume this any more. The Redeemed

---

15. Myunghee Lee, "Migrant Workers Churches as Welcoming, Sending and Recruiting Entities", in Wan and Pocock, eds., 2009. *Missions from the Majority World*, Pasadena, CA: William Carey Library.

Christian Church of God, a Pentecostal denomination from
Nigeria, now has over 800 churches in the UK alone, with
well-developed ministry schools and Bible colleges, discipleship programmes, festivals, and overseas mission programmes.
We are talking about an increasingly mature and self-assured
missionary movement. They do not need Western missionaries to come in and tell them what they need to do.

Fruitfulness in diaspora church planting for sending organizations is contingent upon the ability to
form genuine partnerships with the Majority World
church, and to become servants and learners of those
within the global diaspora. In diaspora missions it is
no longer possible to simply talk about partnerships
with the Majority World church. This is especially
true for Western mission organizations.[16]

Honest partnership with diaspora churches will begin with a
recognition of this context and of our own history. Can we
come to these churches in a spirit of humility, being prepared
to ask what calling God has placed upon *them*, and if there are
ways that we can support them in fulfilling that calling? Are
we prepared to join *their* teams, instead of expecting them
to conform to our image of mission? If so, then there may
be grounds for fruitful partnership. If not, then perhaps our
involvement will do more damage than good.

Where the missionary can help in many diaspora church
situations is as a cultural bridge *within* the church. Diaspora
churches work well for the needs of the first generation of immigrants, who generally operate within the "home" (African,
Latin, etc.) culture. Tensions can then arise between the first

---

16. John Baxter, 2019, *Mobilization and Training for Church Planting in the Global Diaspora*, Evangelical Missions Quarterly 55:1, 30-32.

generation, who see the church as having an important role in preserving the home culture, and the second generation, who have integrated "host" (European) culture into their world-view. Second-generation Nigerians in the UK may prefer to worship in English rather than in Hausa; may have different attitudes to authority structures and formality; and would certainly find it difficult to bring their British friends to a culturally African church.

A culturally-aware missionary, particularly one from a culture which is neither "home" nor "host", can help to navigate these tensions. Because of the issues around conserving the home culture, it is perhaps better to consider working with the mission vision of the second and third generations in order to reach the European indigenes. But this would also require careful awareness of potential difficulties in the power dynamics between these second and third generations and the church leadership.

Diaspora missiology is a burgeoning area of study. In particular there are important discussions of the concept of "reverse mission" and reflections on relationships between diaspora groups, Majority World mission, and Western mission efforts. For reasons of time and space these cannot be summarized here, but those becoming involved with diaspora mission efforts should be careful to be aware of the existing dialogue around these issues.[17]

---

17. See, particularly, material produced by the Lausanne Diaspora Network; Chandler Im and Amos Yong (eds), 2014, *Global Diasporas and Mission*. Oxford: Regnum Books; Israel Olofinjana, 2015, *Partnership in Mission: A Black Majority Church perspective on mission and church unity*, Watford: Instant Apostle; Israel Olofinjana (ed), 2020, *World Christianity in Western Europe: Diaspora Identity, Narratives & Missiology*, Oxford: Regnum Books; Harvey Kwiyani, 2014, *Sent Forth: African Missionary Work in the West*. Maryknoll, NY: Orbis (American Society of Missiology Series).

RESTRUCTURING EXISTING AGENCIES

Many existing mission agencies, including my own, have grown and diversified over the course of their history. And despite the emphasis I have placed in this report on mission being a "mass movement" outside of the professional mission cadre and the need to support expressions of mission which are both trans-organisational and non-organisational in nature, existing agencies and similar structures will continue to be part of the missions movement for the foreseeable future. However, further changes will be required in their operations to enable them to respond to the changes taking place in our society.

TRANS-NATIONAL AND CROSS-NATIONAL BRANCH NETWORK-ING

First, while many agencies are already grasping the reality that mission is indeed "everywhere to everywhere", and allowing for the mission "into" traditional "sending" countries and mission "from" traditional "receiving" countries, this everywhere-to-everywhere approach has generally fallen along the lines of the nation state, with the added assumption that nation state equals ethnic group. So for instance, a mobilizer in Chad might recruit a Chadian worker who has a passion for seeing British people come to faith, and hence send them as a missionary to England.

Flexibility and freedom in the two contexts of sending and receiving is a positive development beyond the old rigid divisions of what constitutes a "sending country" and a "receiving country", but it still fails to take note of the mosaic and transcultural nature of today's world. Do we also see such agencies intentionally mobilizing Iranians in Turkey to reach

Thai people in Germany? On one level, organisational structures must have the flexibility to enable such a "four-context"
understanding of mission. This may well include setting up
teams of missionaries not just for local fellowship, ministry
and accountability, but additionally, four-context missionaries will also belong to transnational teams, sharing experience
and resources between missionaries working with the same
people group, culture and language but dispersed geographi-
cally around the world.

On another level, however, four-context mission must not
merely become a structural *possibility*, but rather a strategic
imperative. Agencies will need to broaden their understanding of recruitment and mobilization practices in order to intentionally seek out those whom God is raising up as missionaries in unexpected places, and also be prepared to guide
them towards perhaps unusual combinations of people group
and location. This will require greater levels of strategic and
contextual awareness both of the "sending" and "receiving"
contexts, but will better serve to enable mission in a mosaic
world.

ENGAGING NON-"MISSIONARIES" IN MISSION

A commitment to partnering with diaspora Christians, as
discussed above, is one aspect of a larger strategic shift that
mission agencies should consider if they are genuinely seeking to reach beyond their own institutional boundaries and
to engage the broader church in mission. A shift in thinking
from production to impact will see traditional missionaries
either working alongside or remotely resourcing overseas foreign workers, students, local churches and Christian communities as part of a wider understanding of what it means to
be a church planting team.

This more catalytical church planting may take place in many forms. In some of these cases, the "professional" missionary may have a clear vision for church planting and, as in the traditional model, be directly involved themselves, evangelising and discipling alongside partners from outside their organisational missionary team. In other cases, they may train, resource and mentor external partners in setting up a church planting effort, without necessarily being directly involved in the work themselves.

But we should be careful not to assume that the church planting impetus should always come from the "professional" missionary. They may find themselves in a situation where a local church or group of Christians have a church planting idea in mind already, and should be open to serving the vision of others either in a direct or in a consultative role.

Alternatively, they may identify a situation where Christians going overseas for whatever reason are eager to take their faith with them and are looking for opportunities of training, resources and mentoring - for example, the situation in which the Phillipines Mission Alliance found themselves. In such a case, the more impactful course of action for such a missionary may be to spend their time resourcing those mission-minded Christians instead of being directly engaged in church planting ministry themselves.

All of this is going to require a paradigm shift from agencies, which will then filter down to individual missionaries: it requires taming the activist drive to "go out and do something", and instead having the situational, strategic and spiritual awareness to stop and first identify and follow up opportunities for catalytical ministry. While I would not recommend that *all* missionaries be encouraged to make this shift, the promotion of a more catalytical approach to ministry, explicitly giving permission to and normalizing "indirect" forms of ministry, and the intentional encouragement of situational surveys and resource audits as part of church planting planning, will all help to generate an expectation that impact is a more useful metric of activity than production.

MEMBERSHIP AND MOBILIZATION MODELS

A consequence of a more catalytical model of ministry will be increased partnerships between those in traditional mission agencies and those outside the agency structures. They will work together, plan together, and worship together; to all intents and purposes they will be on the same "team". But organisationally, they will not be. If the mission agency is to engage with and support those outside of its own structures, and grows in partnerships with external workers, then it will naturally find itself struggling tensions regarding who is "inside" and who is "outside".

At the same time, as will be discussed in the chapter on finance, within the agency we will see varying degrees of commitment and availability. Missionaries will increasingly have to be full-time or part-time employed as a source of support, or otherwise engaged in "visa platform" activities which mean they have commitments to an identity outside that of full-time mission agency member.

In this sense, the concept of "membership" of a mission organisation will experience tension in two directions: there will be those who are on the outside but look as though they are in, and those who are on the inside but look as though they are out. Do we only provide our support and "services" to those who are "in", or is there scope to be generous and include supporting missionaries who are "out"?

Together with our notes on decentralised networks in chapter three, all of this points to the need for a more flexible understanding of mission membership - to see membership in mission sending organisations more along the lines of a "centered set" than a "bounded set"[18], similarly to the transformation of understanding of church membership championed by the missional church movement. Frost and Hirsch explain bounded sets as "fences", where one is either decisively inside or outside, whereas bounded sets are more like "wells", to which a herd of animals will naturally gravitate and identify with. In a church context, this means that formal in-or-out membership status less important than one's "direction of travel" - towards Jesus or away from him. In an agency context, this may mean that agencies commit themselves to serving, mentoring and caring for all mission-minded Christians who desire to associate themselves with that agency for whatever purpose and period.

Similarly, each ministry context should be seen as a mobilization context. Where there are new churches formed through missionary activity, they should be involved in cross-cultural ministry at an early stage. Where there are other churches in the area, particularly those of another ethnic group, they should be mobilized for ministry. The question in catalytic ministry should always be "who else can we involve?"

RENEWED EMPHASIS ON PRAYER

In the first two chapters of this report, we examined the role of Christians in participating in God's mission, and in particular the limitations of human strategy and the need to

---

18. See Paul Hiebert, 1994, *Anthropological Reflections on Missiological Issues*. Grand Rapids, MI: Baker Academic, 123-130, and also Michael Frost and Alan Hirsch, 2013, *The Shaping of Things to Come: Innovation and Mission for the 21st-Century Church*, Grand Rapids, MI: Baker, chapter 3.

respond faithfully to the call of the Holy Spirit - to develop
a tentative plan to "preach the word in the province of Asia",
but yet also be sensitive to when "the Spirit of Jesus would not
allow them to" and alert to the "vision of a man of Macedonia"
(Acts 16:6-9).

The measures outlined above can be seen as the tentative
plan, the application of strategic and organisational thinking
to the situation we find ourselves in. But the mission of God
takes place both in the strategic and in the spiritual realms.
Labourers in the harvest are instructed to pray for more God's
provision of more labourers (Luke 10:2), and congregations
are instructed to pray for church planting teams (Eph 6:19-20,
Col 4:3, 1 Th 5:25); those church planting teams need to be
active in prayer so as to be connected with the vision of God
which reveals changes to the tentative plan.

Within my organisation, we are committed to the value
of prayer as our first core practice, "a priority and integral to
everything we do". Yet the "prayer batteries" which have long
prayed regularly for members are demographically skewed
towards retirees and the elderly. While these groups do have
both the time and the dedication to "pray without ceasing" for
world mission, without an engagement of new generations, it
is difficult to see where how a prayer movement for mission
partners can be sustained.

Prayer for missions and the unreached is still regarded as
a minority activity within the church, rather than as a core
part of the church's mission. A new movement is needed in
three dimensions: to engage the whole church in prayer for
the unreached and to see it as an essential part of what it
means to be church together; to recruit a new demographic
for concerted global prayer for mission; and to encourage and

equip missionaries in their own prayer life so that they are responsive to the Spirit in their own ministries.

CHAPTER SIX
Technology and mission

By the second quarter of 2017, two billion people around the world were actively using Facebook at least once a month; at the time of writing, the figure is 2.4 billion.[1] Where are the unreached? They're on the Internet.

Historically, missionaries have been pioneers in the use of communications technology for the sake of the Gospel. Mission activity drove technological advances. Between 1800 and 1838, the Serampore Mission Press in India made use of their technological expertise in printing and typeface creation to distribute the Gospels in languages and scripts which had never seen printed form before,[2] and even now, organisations such as SIL develop new software to facilitate Bible translation and distribution.

As technology continues to develop ever more rapidly, has missionary activity kept pace? My feeling is that the mission sector has now moved from being *developers* of new technological advance to primarily *users* of existing technologies, and more and more we are slipping behind and failing to make creative use of the technologies available to use in our work.

---

1. https://zephoria.com/top-15-valuable-facebook-statistics/ accessed 19 June 2019.
2. Fiona Ross, 1988, *The Evolution of the Printed Bengali Character from 1778 to 1978* (PhD Thesis, School of Oriental and African Studies), p. 102.

Not that there is anything wrong with primarily being
users, and I am not suggesting that using technology has not
been used to amazing effect for missionary work. Even where
they have not led the development of new technologies, missionaries throughout history have benefited by making use of
the technological advances of others to spread their message:
a common language and an efficient postal service allowed
Paul to communicate with his churches; the development
of the printing press enabled the cheap and easy distribution of millions of copies of the Bible; radio, television and
film ministry (in particular the Jesus Film) have brought the
Gospel to millions; and now through the Internet, missionaries can mentor and disciple their contacts from anywhere in
the world with face-to-face video calls over platforms such as
Skype or Zoom.

But is there more that we can do? Even in 1990, before
the Internet became ubiquitous, mission leaders were calling
for missionaries to make every effort to harness new technologies in the service of the Gospel:

The information age that has dawned is an age in
which the explosion of the gospel ought to super-
sede that of the first century. Everything is now in
place which should enable Christians to gossip the
good news of the gospel to all of the peoples of the
world... The world has come into the information
arena where we as Christians have lived all of our
history. This is who we are. If we would but rec-
ognize and be wise enough, sacrificial enough, and
creative enough, we will move into the greatest day

Christian missions has ever seen.[3]

Significant ministries at present include Sat 7, which is rapidly establishing itself as "best practice" for Christian satellite TV outreach / discipleship; the use of targeted advertisements on social media to create leads for evangelism; using social media for discipleship and mentoring[4]; and the Mobile Minstry Forum, which is a network of over 900 individuals from 125 different ministries, dedicated to developing tools and resourcing mission thorugh mobile devices. Other organisations such as Kingdom Code bring together programmers with an interest in developing tools for Christian ministry but are not specifically related to cross-cultural mission.

WHAT'S MISSING

There are no magic bullets in mission, and while technology can be a helpful tool to be used (and developed) for the kingdom of God, technological solutions are only part of a broader picture of what is needed in mission today.

For one thing, technology will not reach everyone; despite the 2.3 billion monthly users of Facebook, the World Economic Forum estimates that half of the world's population is still not connected to the Internet.[5] (The International Telecommunication Union estimates that as of 2019, 53.6% of the world's population were using the Internet, but that 97% are within reach of a mobile Internet signal.)[6]

---

3. Keith Parks, 1990, *The Information Age and World Missions are Made for Each Other* (Richmond: Southern Baptist Foreign Mission Board, Accession number 571, December 10, 1990).
4. See e.g. Vance Brown, 2012, *An Analysis of the Strategic Use of Technology-Based Services, Including Social Networking Services, As More Effective and Complete Tools for Christians to Fulfil the Great Commission*, MBA Thesis, IGlobal University.
5. https://www.weforum.org/agenda/2018/05/half-the-world-s-population-is-still-offline-heres-why-that-matters
6. https://www.itu.int/en/ITU-D/Statistics/Pages/facts/default.aspx

Although this will continue to change as technology increases its penetration around the world, access to the Gospel should not be determined by access to technology. In some parts of the world, face-to-face evangelism and discipleship will remain the only way to do mission. Even where technologically mediated communication is available, there are reasons why it should only be used as a supplement to personal interaction rather than the primary means of mission.

CONNECTING THE CODERS

One of the best things about using technology in mission is that you can harness the skills and passion of people all over the world, without them needing to go overseas full-time. Coders in Rio de Janeiro and Lagos can use their skills in service of the Gospel, working together to build tools to reach and disciple people in India, and do all this for a few hours a day after work or at weekend "hackfests". But this advantage comes paired with a disadvantage – how much do you lose by not actually being there on the ground?

Of course, it depends on how well these digital evangelists are linked to knowledge of the local context, and in particular, how contextually aware they are in developing their resources. Some organisations are aware of this challenge and responding appropriately, while others are still working out how best to do this. I feel in general, however, that there is still a need for closer networking between digital workers and local pastors and evangelists, so that information flow can be improved in two directions.

The first direction where improved information flow is needed is from the "digital world" to the local context. When contacts and leads are generated through Internet evangelism, it is easy to continue the conversation through the Internet platform; but it is more difficult to identify appropriate local Christians who can maintain the discipleship relationship with face-to-face interaction. Even if the situation demands that the relationship continues purely in the digital sphere (say in situations of persecution), with improved networking between a local ministry context and the digital platforms, it should be possible for the technology platform to intermediate questions about discipleship or about Christianity which are culture-specific with people who have more of an awareness or understanding of their particular context.

Doing this would require navigating conversations about "ownership" of leads and disciples, and about the selection of who is "appropriate" as a local point of contact - two questions which are admittedly often difficult to resolve in practice. But from a perspective of idealism, having each denomination or ministry developing their own online evangelism platform, connected (as best) with whatever contacts they have on the ground in particular areas, is both wasteful and scattershot. If we get to a place where church and para-church organisations can network and learn to trust one another, we can better serve those reached through Internet evangelism with local connection. Another implication of this, that will be considered later, is that Internet evangelism and discipleship should be coupled with real-world community.

The other direction of information flow which could be improved is the communication from local to digital, in terms of having local workers on the ground feeding into the development processes of digital missionaries. This is necessary to help determine what resources are created in the first place: on-the-ground missionaries and pastors can guide the development of apps and resources which applicable to their cultural contexts, and provide ideas that those remote to the context cannot be expected to come up with. It is also necessary to provide appropriate contextualisation of the resources which are generated remotely.

It appears that, in many cases, remote developers begin "generic" discipleship resources, often created in the West, and then translate them remotely (sometimes even using machine translation) into target languages. These target languages may not be the most contextually appropriate for a particular people group - for example, using modern standard Arabic across Arabic-speaking contexts instead of translating into local Arabic vernaculars, let alone using local and tribal languages. Beyond choice of translation language, there is also often little adaptation of the materials to the worldviews and needs of the local context. The input of local workers and leaders can therefore be invaluable to present evangelism and discipleship in ways that resonate with cultural and local needs.

This highlights a very real need in the sphere of digital evangelism right now; both of these areas can be improved with a determined effort to coordinate and network between existing groups of digital missionaries, and by providing a forum through which these digital missionaries can interact with local partners. Facilitating such networking and conversation would dramatically increase the scope and applicability of Internet-based evangelism efforts.

CREATING COMMUNITY

I write this over Easter from a country in lockdown due to the COVID-19 pandemic. All over the world, churches have had to very quickly discover new ways of being church without meeting physically. While some churches have simply streamed their existing worship services in a one-way, broadcast modality, the pandemic experience has also forced many churches to develop ways of connecting online as a two-way interactive community: for example, using videoconferencing for virtual house groups and prayer meetings, and creating WhatsApp and Facebook groups for sharing news and prayer online.

The lack of physical community has heightened the need for connection, and this need has found expression through the Internet. It remains to be seen how these local church communities will continue to develop their Internet-based discipleship presence once the lockdown is over and physical meetings can resume again, but we can imagine a greater synergy between online and offline: online Christian communities but related to and emerging from distinct local and physical church communities.

Compare this, however, with the typical model of Internet-based mission, which assumes an individualistic mentality: a lead is generated and connected for one-to-one follow-up with either a remote or, less often, a local discipler. But the Christian faith finds its expression not in one-to-one relationships, in the context of the Church, the Christian community; this is something that majority communitarian cultures already understand and appreciate. Again, while there are certainly cases where, for reasons of safety or fear of official or unofficial persecution, one-to-one discipleship is the most appropriate, in the vast majority of cases, the process of discipleship and Christian growth is itself facilitated through interaction with the Christian community. After all, Jesus left us not a book or a set of rules but primarily a community.

Some Internet discipleship programmes are moving from a one-to-one to a discipleship community model, but more can be done to stress the importance of community when building discipleship platforms. At the same time, more could be done to explore the possibilities of building bridges between physical church communities and online mission: both in terms of how Internet community can support existing local churches, as we are currently seeing in the coronavirus lockdown, and how those primarily being discipled online can be "plugged in" to local churches through the Internet.

THEOLOGICAL IMPLICATIONS

The final area in which the technological aspect of mission can be developed is a theological one, which actually underlies both of the areas we have already discussed. Those producing, resourcing and coordinating Internet evangelism would benefit from facilitated theological reflection on their practice, because I believe that technologically-mediated Christianity and mission produces some distinctive theological issues. I have already mentioned how content generation raises questions of translation and contextualization, which have been part of the misisological discourse for decades, but there are other areas in which greater theological reflection would improve mission practice.

Before becoming a missionary, I worked as a computer programmer, and still am involved in programming. And yet I find it difficult to get excited about Internet evangelism, particularly some of the models based on advertising and web-based broadcast messaging. When I stop to ask myself why, I find myself reflecting on the nature of the incarnation and its relationship to witness. The incarnation speaks not just of a message to be broadcast and a truth to be conveyed, but of a message which is embodied within and inseparable from the life of a messenger. Jesus was both the message and the medium, and the medium was personal. This again demonstrates the need for human community in the Christian mission experience.

The problem is that Internet-mediated Gospel message is necessarily disembodied from the life of the messenger, because what is communicated is deliberate and curated; the evangelist selects carefully what to share about their life - even seemingly impromptu thoughts and posts can be part of a deliberate process of messaging, and it is almost impossible for people to see the kind of genuinely unscheduled reactions to events that really reveals a person's character.

In other words, there is a discussion to be had as to what extent evangelism without presence can be used to either supplement or replace traditional means of "going" in mission. Similarly, there is a need for reflection on the nature of technology itself in the Christian enterprise; the Japanese theologian Kosuke Koyama, for example, produced a series of meditations[7] on the subject of how "technological thinking" - with its values of efficiency, abstract, and impersonality - can pervert the Christian Gospel.

All this is not to say that Internet evangelism is an inappropriate means of witness; what I am trying to say is that the use of technology in mission needs to be carefully thought through in theological terms so that these kind of questions can be answered in a satisfying way. Developing training resources and fora for discussion of the theological implications of technology-mediated mission will be a helpful

---

7.   Kosuke Koyama, 1976, *No Handle on the Cross: An Asian Meditation on the Crucified Mind*. SCM Press: London.

way of improving the missionary quality of these kinds of resources.

CONCLUSIONS

Technological advances provide many opportunities for innovative mission practices, and their use will only increase as we continue towards greater penetration of Internet use. However, these opportunities bring with them a distinct set of challenges. We have identified that there is a place for further development in the practice of Internet evangelism and discipleship, in a number of respects.

First, there is a need to develop greater feedback loops between developers and field workers, to ensure that material created is appropriate for mission contexts and that those in the field are able to request development of apps and websites to supplement their on-the-ground activities, as well as to provide physical and local networks for those reached through Internet evangelism. Creating such networks would best be done by a consortium of churches and mission organisations, representing as wide a spread as possible of developers, content producers and designers as well as local Christian workers, national and foreign.

There is also a need to extend Internet efforts into the physical world by providing on-line connections between members of physical Christian communities, as well as rooting those reached on-line into an expression of the body of Christ local to them. At the same time, Internet evangelism and discipleship needs to find ways to break out of the one-to-one approach and create discipling communities, both on-line and off.

Finally, with cross-organisational fora in place to connect the various people and organisations working in the Internet evangelism space, it would also be beneficial to facilitate a greater depth of theological and missiological reflection on practice - particularly on the areas of contextualization, translation, incarnation, and the impact of technology on worldview - so that materials produced by digital missionaries are not merely expedient and efficient but are also authentic expressions of a missional Christian faith.

CHAPTER SEVEN

The money issue

The "Carey model" of mission upon which traditional Western mission sending structures is based is, essentially, a *financial* model. Being founded explicitly on the basis of the limited stock company, the Western mission model assumes a missionary who is (1) operating full-time in a dedicated "ministerial" role, and (2) supported by subscriptions from overseas. While some sectors of the mission community have experimented with alternative funding models, the fundamental model remains essentially unchallenged.

However, there are reasons why this model should be challenged in this current context.

CHALLENGES TO THE EXISTING MODEL

The first of the assumptions we highlighted in the Carey model is that missionaries are a dedicated, full-time and elite force. Indeed, in his *Enquiry*, Carey writes about the need for selection and investigation of the views of potential missionaries to ensure that they are of sufficient calibre and character for the task. From the start of the modern Protestant mission movement, mission was seen as the preserve of the few, not the many, and there was little interest in involving the whole of the Church in mission. The financial model was therefore based on a distinction between "professional" missionaries and "other" Christians, who were not regarded as missionaries and would remain at home purely in a supporting role. If, on the other hand, we are interested in seeing the whole Church involved in mission, we will need to erase the distinction between "supporter" and "supported", and open the way to alternative models beyond overseas support.

Because of their financial support, those counted as a professional missionaries in the Carey model were free to spend their entire time and labour in Christian ministry (and specifically, evangelism). Even at the start of the modern Protestant mission movement, medical missions and other "mercy ministries" were consider appropriate missionary activities alongside "pure" evangelism and church planting. Yet within that, the missionary was still expected to be master of their own time and schedule, and the financial model provided the missionary this freedom. As Carey put it,

> A Christian minister is a person who in a peculiar sense is not his own; he is the servant of God, and therefore ought to be wholly devoted to him. By entering on that sacred office he solemnly undertakes to be always engaged, as much as possible, in the Lord's work, and not to chuse his own pleasure, or employment, or pursue the ministry as a something that is to subserve his own ends, or interests, or as a kind of bye-work.

Yet a full-time missionary vocation should not be regarded as *a priori* the most appropriate one for ministry. It is equally fair to say that the "professional" missionary - in terms of a full-time evangelist or church planter - is a strange and often unrelatable anomaly, and certainly provides a poor model for new Christians in an "unreached" community. One reason given for the poor spread of the Gospel in Japan has been that "professional" missionaries have little access to working men, and the men in turn have few examples of how the faith they are hearing about is worked out in practice.[1] Those involved in business as mission have therefore found that their business operations affords them with an identity as a working person that is viewed with less suspicion than that of "missionary", as well as providing a much more natural source of connections to customers, clients and staff than those in full time church-planting ministry who can often spend much of their time generating artificial opportunities to build relationships and friendships with those around them.

At the same time, the second assumption - that missionaries should be supported by subscriptions from "home" - was born in a context of affluent Western Christianity, which is no longer appropriate now that the majority of overseas missionaries come from the non-Western world:

> [The personal/denominational support model] does depend on a sending context with the capacity to raise the significant sums of money involved in supporting work overseas. It worked for mission from an affluent context, but is something else when mission comes from less affluent contexts. The difficulty can be exacerbated by differing expectations when people work together in mission teams from very different socio-economic contexts."[2]

The vulnerable missions movement[3] is righly challenging the

---

1. Dowsett 2005, "Gender Imbalance in East Asian Churches", *Mission Round Table* 1:4, 27.
2. Paul Bendor-Samuel, 2017. "Challenge and realignment in the Protestant cross-cultural mission movement". *Transformation*, 34(4):273.
3. See e.g. Harries, 2011, *Vulnerable Mission: Insights Into Christian Mission to Africa*, Pasadena, CA: William Carey Library.

whole concept of ministering while reliant on external resources on both theological and practical grounds. But even
movements such as the Alliance for Vulnerable Mission assume that although the *ministry* should use local resources,
the *missionary* may be funded from overseas. As Eleanor
Hof's critique[4] points out, while claiming to be post-colonial in outlook this still represents a Western-centric view
of mission. For the perspective missionary from a relatively
poor context, the model of personal support from overseas
may not even be attainable - consider a situation where a
missionary's living expenses in their country of service are
five or ten times the salary of the pastor in their home church!
These missionaries can have no choice but to be vulnerable in
the sense of relying on local resources not just for ministry
expenses but also for living expenses.

These topics are often further clouded by a resistance to
open discussions about money and personal support in missions, perhaps driven in places by cultural reticence, and in
others by a conservative and simplistic understanding of the
"faith principle" in missions. In traditional "faith missions",
"people were challenged to go without any financial guarantees, simply trusting that the Lord of mission would provide."[5]
However, this emphasis on faith in God's provision only really extended in practice to provision *through personal support
donations*. This again drives a wedge between the professional
missionary and the everyday experience of mission-minded
Christians.

4.   Eleanora Hof, 2016, *Reimagining Mission in the Postcolonial Condition A Theology of
     Vulnerability and Vocation at the Margins*, PhD thesis: Protestant Theological University of
     Amsterdam, 188-194.
5.   David Bosch, 1991. *Transforming mission: Paradigm shifts in theology of mission*.
     Maryknoll, NY: Orbis, 333.

While respecting the faith principle, perhaps a wider view of faith is needed which stresses human reliance on God's provision for all areas of life - all of us rely on God's provision of "the rains in their time so that the land will give its yield" (Lev 26:4), in the sense that there are resources which we need for our sustenance which are beyond our own ability to control: on the one hand, continued financial donations for those receiving traditional personal support, but on the other, continued health and economic stability for those employed or self-employed. Recognising God's provision of all of the externalities of life both recognises the need for faith amongst the "non-professional" as well as the "professional" missionary, and opens the way for "professional" missionaries to trust God for financial provision in non-traditional ways.

POTENTIAL SOLUTIONS

What options are there beyond the ministerial model? Some, such as business as mission and missionary "tentmaking", are accepted to varying degrees as missionary expressions. But are there alterative financial models than can be explored?

BUSINESS AS MISSION

Business as mission has emerged as a key means of allowing missionaries to self-support and gain access to mission fields, and has a wide range of benefits: as mentioned already, it provides a relatable identity and the ability to demonstrate faith in an everyday context. It creates natural relationships through customers and clients, and provides the employer-missionary with a way to demonstrate their faith in action at close quarters through the way that they treat staff and resolve problems on a day-to-day basis. It may also be the only way for missionaries to access certain "closed" countries.

But despite these advantages, business as mission must not be regarded as a "magic bullet" solution to the problem of mission funding. This is not, as Carey would argue, due to the corrupting effect of business upon mission activity. For one thing, even with the best advice and support, business as mission in a church planting context requires that a missionary be both a competent church planter and a competent and enterpreneurial businessperson. This does not suit the temperaments or the gifts of all.

More problematically, just as the traditional "professional missionary" role often means that the missionary only relates to those that they serve in a context of religious teaching, with all the power dynamics that this implies, the business-man witnesses to their employees in the context of the employer-employee power differential. Even when the business-man is witnessing to clients, customers, or peers, what is being demonstrated is Christianity "from above" - Christianity associated with power and affluence. Once again, the form of Christianity that is modelled is an aspirational one, not the Christianity of the masses.

LOCAL WORK, FOREIGN FUNDS?

With an affluent but increasingly non-missionary Western church and a vibrant missionary community amongst the less affluent churches, one potential solution would be for the West to supply the funds and the rest to supply the people. Indeed, one approach to mission which is becoming increasingly prevalent amongst churches in the UK is to fund projects operated and staffed by local workers. In one sense, this can be seen as a genuine partnership, with each side giving out of the resources it has available. However, as in the case of business as mission, money is not merely a resource, but also a proxy for power, and an unbalanced power dynamic does not make for a partnership of equals.

At the same time, even though the West does have the money, a reliance on funding from outside sources tends towards the kind of dependency which robs local workers of their agency and their chance to develop into self-sustaining missions movements:

> The prevailing theory is that the more affluent nations need to propel this giant forward with outside funding. In our opinion, unless this paradigm is challenged and changed, at both ends, no long lasting change with result. The West can and should contribute in appropriate ways. But the needed income for the emerging missions movement will only become sustainable as their leaders develop internal systems that generate core funds.[6]

There are also questions about the effectiveness of foreign funding of missions. Internal critiques of the Seed Company's approach to providing foreign funding for local Bible translation have hinged upon the fact that projects become funded on the basis of their ability to satisfy the expectations of foreign donors - exciting proposals, eye-catching reports, and an emphasis on impressive-sounding statistics - rather than on the true quality of translation and effectiveness of operations.

For these reasons, Western funding of majority world missions seems to be a stop-gap which mitigates the financial

---

6. Howard Brant, 2009, "Seven Essentials of Majority World Emerging Mission Movements", in Wan and Pocock, eds., *Missions from the Majority World*, Pasadena, CA: William Carey Library, 50.

disparity in missions while bringing a number of problems of its own, rather than a genuinely new "revolution in world missions".[7]

BIVOCATIONAL MISSION

Questions of missionary finance very quickly become intertwined with questions of membership and identity. What I mean by that is that the acceptance of business as mission as a legitimate missional expression already moves us beyond the expectation that the missionary is a dedicated, full-time minister of the Gospel. And if we are to accept that a missionary can further the Gospel while running a business, then surely a missionary can also further the Gospel while involved in other occupations - or to put it another way, someone involved in other occupations can also be a minster of the Gospel. Indeed for many, the only realistic way to access and maintain a life in another country will be as a migrant worker, international student or similar, and doing so can be a better way to develop natural networks of relationships than entering as a dedicated "professional" missionary.

In traditional agencies, this has only been available for those ministering in "creative access" countries, with those who are able to enter a country in a full-time ministerial role able to do so. But this has in turn caused difficulties around the subject of identity - a missionary must maintain two faces, separating their "visa platform" identity in country from their missionary identity to their organisation and friends and supporters back home, with the resulting anxiety that such identities should ever be conflated.

---

7. See also Douglas Rutt, 2001, *Hiring National Missionaries: A Good Idea?* Lutheran Missiology.

Were we to understand the role of migrant worker Christian or overseas student Christian as a legitimate missionary expression of faith, then the identity issues goes away; one is not a missionary pretending to be a language student, but a genuine language student who is a Christian and is therefore a missionary.

Of course, we are in an age where many people besides professional missionaries are accessing and maintaining a life in another country as a matter of course, and taking their faith with them as they do so. For example, the Phillipines Mission Alliance, together with the Phillipines Missions Mobilization Movement, have adopted this broader view of vocation and mission, and challenged Filipinos Christians overseas to see themselves as tentmaking missionaries:

> PMA hosts training programs both in the Philippines and abroad among Filipinos about to work overseas or are already working there. These training programs are designed to slowly bring Filipino evangelicals to a realization that they could have a higher purpose in working abroad and the commitment to pursue this purpose.[8]

It is worth mentioning that the Philippines has the third highest number of overseas workers in the world, behind Mexico and India, and so these programmes are a necessary theological response to a particular "Overseas Foreign Worker" phenomenon. But in another sense, the Philippine missions movement is at the leading edge of a situation that many other nations now find themselves in - having to think about the role of the missionary in a context of increased labour

---

8. Joseph Cruz, 2013. *Faith in Exile: Evangelical Communities and Filipino Migrant Workers*, Master's Thesis, National University of Singapore.

migration. In such a context, the distinction between "missionary" and "mission minded Christian" is quite fine, and this is very welcome if one of our goals is to engage the whole Church in mission.

Indeed, the only practical difference between a migrant worker who is a missionary and a migrant worker who is a mission-minded Christian is the amount of mentoring, training, resources and peer support available from a mission support organisation. As well as allowing for mission workers to take a bivocational approach in open access countries as well as creative access countries, can existing agencies open up their membership to provide such support more broadly to overseas workers and students - as the Phillipines Mission Alliance has demonstrated - or do we need to establish some kind of "mission agency for non-missionaries", which provides such support services not on the basis of membership but based on the need to support the whole world Christian movement in its missional expression?

In either case, finding ways to support the many migrant Christians around the world, encouraging them to see themselves as bivocational missionaries, and enabling them with the resources to do so, seems to be an important path in the development of mission beyond the professional, ministerial model, and would merit considerable further investment.

INCOME GENERATION

Another potential approach would be for sending structures to facilitate, either directly or indirectly, income generation as a means of support for missionaries and local workers.

One team within my own agency is mobilizing missionaries from Africa, and is approaching the funding problem by training the candidates in income generation through small-scale farming techniques. These projects are designed to be culturally appropriate in the missionaries' areas of service and to require relatively low start-up costs. Another endeavour aims to provide missionaries with ready-made small businesses in the form of mushroom cultivation containers. These speciality mushrooms can be grown almost anywhere, and either sold locally if demand is sufficient or through food markets in more affluent areas.

These examples raise two important points: First, time and effort spent developing new models of support can enable many more workers to be active in cross-cultural ministry. An enterpreneur or businessperson dedicated to support provision can therefore fulfil a legitimate and useful missionary support role. Second, they also highlight a potential role for traditional mission agencies or para-mission structures in providing wider support for income generation efforts. There are various ways in which this support could be provided. In agencies which have embraced business as mission, there are often business consultants who are available - either full time or part time - to support BAM efforts and projects. Dedicated consultants, either internal or external to an agency, can assist missionaries, particularly those from low-income background, by developing these kinds of income generation ideas and "packages" to enable them to become self-supporting.

The international nature of many mission supporting structures such as the traditional agencies also raises the possibility of access to global markets; a Nigerian missionary growing speciality mushrooms in a shipping container in Cambodia can, with the connections provided by an international mission agency or mission support organisation, ship her products to a Singaporean colleague for onward sale to the restaurant trade.

The idea of using mission support structures as, essentially, global trading companies would provoke serious and necessary reservations from a perspective of postcolonialist critique, and it may be that the colonialist associations would prove impossible to overcome. But providing the power dynamics could be structured with these concerns in mind, using the levers of globalisation to enable greater participation of the majority world in mission may be an important and useful subversion of the colonialist trope.

Another approach which builds on this and the wider access to the Internet is the possiblity of teleworking as an income generation strategy. I spoke to a missionary who is investigating the use of a data entry microbusiness to support new Christians who have been obstracized from family and employment; similar teleworking arrangements could be provided as a part-time income for missionaries. Developing viable businesses would be a valuable contribution to global mission, and agencies would benefit from identifying people either inside or outside of their structures who are able to create such opportunities.

FLEXIBILITY IN SENDING STRUCTURES

Responding to these new approaches to mission finance will require a considerable degree of flexibility from traditional sending organisations.

For one thing, older "faith" missions may struggle with a widening of the understanding of reliance on God. Missionaries with long experience of the personal support model will have testimonies of God's miraculous financial provision in their own lives, and may see those coming into mission with alternative models as not being prepared to rely fully on God in the same way that they did. Western missionaries in particular may not fully appreciate how much their experience of God's faithfulness is situated within the wider context of an affluent and established mission sending environment. Pastoral sensitivity, and an explicit understanding of what we mean by "faith" in the context of mission, will need to be developed to keep diverse mission contexts united.

Allowing for multiple models of missionary vocation within the same organisation or group of missionaries - traditionally supported and hence "full-time" ministerial, self-employed, employed, student, and so on - raises important questions about the boundaries between "agency member" and non-member. To what degree must one be "fully committed" (in terms of time and availability) to a missionary team in order to be part of it? To make decisions within it? To lead it? Organisations will need to answer these questions themselves, but in keeping with a desire to widen the scope of mission beyond the professional missionary, it would be sensible to move towards greater openness. However, teams which find themselves unable (perhaps for security reasons) to widen their membership criteria may wish to adopt stratified models of membership, perhaps with an "inner core" and "outer core"; this will also be needed when engaging with local Christians and churches as partners and team members.

Finally, explicit team training will be needed to handle different vocational models of mission together in the same team. Teams have always had to handle different levels of support, but have (with the possible exception of language students) generally been able to rely on full availability and commitment. A wider diversity of funding models and levels

together with a range of "outside" commitments will place
further strains on mission team unity - scheduling meetings,
the expenses of social times, expectations of longer times together (such as team conferences), will all need to be adjusted
in a diverse team climate. Missions leadership should advise
teams on how to handle these expectations.

CONCLUSIONS

We have seen that the question of missionary finance
is intimately tied with the question of how we define "missionary" - functionally, a missionary has been traditionally
defined as someone who is in full-time Christian ministry
through overseas financial support. But realising that this
model has severe limitations when it comes to mission partners from less affluent contexts not only leads to a search
for alternative mission models; it also causes us to question
the distinction between a "tentmaking missionary" and a missional migrant worker.

If indeed it turns out there is no such distinction, then
it would make sense for mission sending organisations to either extend their concepts of membership to include migrant
workers, or to ensure that there is equivalent provision for
the mentoring, training and support of foreign workers who
are seeking to share the Gospel in their daily lives.

Even if we define a missionary as someone who belongs
to a mission organisation or who is sent specifically for the
purposes of mission activity by a church or similar sending
context, there is still a need for these organisations to explore
non-traditional sources of support: business as mission and
bivocational models are of some use, but they can be usefully
supplemented by intentional development of microbusiness
and other income generation projects.

CHAPTER EIGHT
The Mission Catalyst

One of the questions we've faced in this journey of re-thinking mission has been "what comes after mission agency?" What this means is, is the Western cross-cultural mission agency as we know it the most suitable vehicle for supporting mission today, and if not, what should be a more suitable vehicle? This chapter presents an alternative approach to structuring missionary activity, which I am calling the *mission catalyst*.

A CHANGING WORLD

We've seen in previous chapters that there are a number of trends in the world today which speak to the need for a new model of mission. Let's briefly summarize those trends once again:

- *Non-Western mission*. While majority world missionaries have always contributed to the mission movement, the past fifty years have seen explosive growth in the number of majority world missionaries and mission agencies. Looking into the future, we can expect the number of new non-Western missionaries to quickly outpace recruitment from the Western world. (Assuming it has not done so already!) These newer agencies and mission sending churches bring energy, enthusiasm, sacrifice and faith to the missionary task and, in many cases, have much to teach us practically, organisationally, and theologically. But they are also often looking for relational connections to the wider mission movement for partnership, training, and support.

- *Increasing fragmentation and direct sending.* In a way, the situation in Western mission is not too different; rather than relying on large, monolithic agencies, missionaries are increasingly going independently or being sent directly through their churches. People do not want to do mission through a middle-man, partly because of the postmodern mistrust of the large institutional organization, but also because moving across the world and living in a different country has become a more accessible undertaking than it has historically been. More agencies are being established, often to support a small group or even individual units in mission. Rather than experience being pooled within an organization, experience is either shared through informal network relationships - or more often, people are making their own mistakes!

- *Financial pressures.* In both Western and non-Western cases, we are seeing a new approach to the issue of money in mission. The traditional model of mission, with "home end" supporters providing 100% of the full-time field missionaries' living expenses, worked well in a relatively affluent Western context. But for the majority world missionary, such an understanding of mission finance becomes a barrier to involvement. Instead of a fully-supported model, they go as either entrepreneurs or migrant workers, working overseas and making their living from the financial resources of the host people.

- *Changing understanding of mission*. Similarly, in the West, younger missionaries are questioning the secular/sacred divide implied in an understanding of the missionary that is dedicated and full-time; for many of them, cross-cultural mission work is a matter of applying one's God-given skills and gifts in a foreign context.

- *The importance of the* missio dei. A recognition that mission belongs to God has changed the way that mission agencies think about strategy. Rather than directing and coordinating, the focus is becoming more on discerning what God is doing and encouraging people to find their place in His activity.

THE NEW NEEDS

Whether these trends are positive or negative, a new way of doing mission and understanding mission seems to be emerging and requires new forms of administrative and organizational support. Let us now think about what kind of support is going to be needed:

- Churches and smaller agencies, both from the majority world and the West, are not looking for another organization to be part of but would still benefit by being linked in to a wider view of mission. This will include hearing about other opportunities and teams where their missionaries are working, and being able to meet others nearby for fellowship and support.

- At the same time, while they do not want another organization to be part of, they do want people to relate to: people who will take an interest in them, be supportive, and offer a listening ear to them. They want experienced and wise counselors who will mentor them in their mission journey.

- Newer churches and agencies are often eager to learn how to train and support their missionaries better and how to better "serve as senders". They are looking for access to training opportunities and people who will help to build their own training capacity. They want the feeling of responsibility to send their own missionaries directly, but the ability to draw on the wisdom and experience of experienced mission senders.

- As mission movements fragment, the administrative overheads increase. Each smaller organization is responsible for providing some kind of administrative and technical support system for their workers, and each organization ends up building their own best practices: ten new organizations means ten new safeguarding policies, ten new IT systems, ten new financial systems, and so on. They would benefit from a range of help on the administrative side, from support and knowledge of best practices through to outsourcing these areas to an external body with specialist experience.

- As the understanding of mission finance changes, and particularly with less affluent countries becoming more active in mission, there is a need to provide financial support and management for mission projects. This may involve "matchmaking" between missionaries and donors, and also providing support for business-as-mission projects.

THE MISSION CATALYST

What I am proposing is a new structure for mission support called the "mission catalyst". The mission catalyst will be a small team of dedicated support workers, consisting of highly networked "connectors", mentors, and training coordinators. Their job is to resource and support these emerging mission movements, as well as providing mentoring for missionaries and connection between different mission projects. Specifically, they will work in the following seven areas:

Connecting people to resources and peers. A mission catalyst can work catalytically to form and resource teams, provide and facilitate fellowship opportunities on the field, and "get the right people in the room together".

Building partnerships with emerging/emerged movements. The mission catalyst will facilitate lateral connections between movements, both new and old, and encourage them to multiply their efforts through partnership together.

Training and equipping. The catalyst may or may not be directly involved in training themselves, as there are plenty of other organizations involved in the sphere, but they will certainly be aware of what training is available in different contexts. They will be responsible for offering access to appropriate training to agencies and missionaries, and for building agencies' capacity for training, both for field missionaries and their sending contexts. This doesn't necessarily mean formal classroom courses – although it may in some cases; the key word is "appropriate" – and will include both in-service and pre-field training.

Arranging technical and structural backup. In an increasingly technologically connected world, field missionaries can supplement their ministry with apps, social media, web sites and so on - but only if they are connected with developers and technical support staff. The catalyst can help field missionaries and technologists with a passion for mission to develop projects which would benefit each other. The catalyst would also help agencies to develop member care best practices, IT security and opsec arrangements, child protection policies, and so on; they would be aware of opportunities to outsource administrative elements of the mission agency and be able to connect organizations with external consultancies (for example, Stewardship) who could help bear the administrative burden.

Financial support and management. Catalysts can help to connect donors with mission projects, particularly when providing start-up or seed funding. They can also act as intermediaries or "expectation translators" to help donors and missionaries understand each other in terms of expectations about what reporting and accountability should look like, what due diligence should be done, and how much involvement and control the donors should be able to exercise.

Mobilizing others into mission. Anyone passionate about mission mobilizes others. A catalyst should always be finding opportunities to call, challenge, mentor and encourage others to explore their own place in God's mission. They may direct people into traditional agencies, or they may encourage local churches to send their own members into mission directly with the support of the mission catalysts. But they will certainly be raising the profile of mission, as well as raising prayer for the nations and for missionaries, to bring more of the Church "from the touchlines onto the playing field."

Mentoring, resourcing and encouraging. The core of a mission catalyst's work will be walking with others in mission: being a sounding board, a resource point, an ally, and a cheerleader. Prayer too will be a central part of this aspect; every Joshua on the field needs a Moses on the mountain. They should be regularly checking in with missionaries they are "connected" to and offering opportunities for input and accountability. Precisely because they are a neutral third party, missionaries can use the catalyst to objectively talk through issues which they may not be able to share directly with their sending organizations or churches.

WHAT WOULD IT LOOK LIKE?

Let's now see some examples of how a mission catalyst might operate. The catalysts in our story, José, Marcus, and Faith, form the East Asia team of a new organization called Walking Together.

TEAM FORMATION

Anil and Neesha, from North East India, have a vision for a new work in Kunming, China. They have recruited another family from their church, Jakob and Lal. Their church is eager to send them but cannot support them financially, so Anil and Jakob are planning to open a restaurant.

A Walking Together catalyst visited the church last year as part of a mobilization tour and talked with Anil and Neesha, and so the elders suggested that Anil contact WT to discuss their plan. José meets with the four potential missionaries. José knows of two other missionaries hoping to start a church in Kunming; David, who is with an American mission agency, and Cherry, who moved to Kunming from Chengdu. At this stage, José isn't sure if the Indian missionaries will work well with David and Cherry, but thinks they should still be aware of each other and get together for fellowship.

José also talks to the church elders to determine what support they would need in order to send the four workers. José takes them through current best practices for missionary sending and helps the church and the missionaries to set expectations together. The church feels comfortable sending the missionaries themselves but wants to learn more about member care, so José agrees to connect the church with local training partners who can teach them about this issue.

Finally, José helps the missionaries think through the practicalities of moving to Kunming. He encourages the church to ensure that they have had good cultural and biblical orientation and provides them with some options for training. The church asks if Walking Together could provide the cultural orientation for them. José arranges for Faith, WT's lead trainer, to come and facilitate these sessions. As Anil and Jakob have not started a business before, José puts them in touch with Marcus, WT's BAM consultant, to give them general advice about business as mission and also to network with other missionaries involved in BAM in China.

Anil and Jakob talk with Marcus, and through his connections, they have held a Skype call with a missionary elsewhere in China who has opened a coffee shop. They are starting to realize that opening a restaurant will require navigating a lot of Chinese bureaucracy. Marcus also contacts a group of businessmen in Singapore who provide seed money for missional coffee shops to see if they would be interested in funding the restaurant. He also works his contacts, to see if any churches or funding bodies would provide the families with money for food and rent for their first six months while they are getting established.

Faith contacts the church eldership and talks about the cultural training that WT can deliver. She asks for one of the elders, Thomas, to be available to assist and co-teach, and provides some material for him to study in advance. She hopes that the next time a local church sends missionaries, Thomas will be able to teach the material without her.

Two months later, Faith comes to India and spends a week with the four missionaries. Together with Thomas, they talk with the candidates about issues of worldview, adaptation, contextualization, and other cultural factors. Faith discovers that Neesha is beginning to feel worried about her ability to learn Chinese and integrate into a different culture.

But the four are still excited, and Faith seems convinced that they understand the issues involved in working overseas, so she recommends to the church that they make arrangements to go to the field. José contacts Cherry and asks if she would be willing to help them find them apartments to rent.

ARRIVAL

In March, the church officially sends them out as missionaries to China. Their first two weeks in the country are a roller-coaster ride: they are excited and eager to start out in mission, but culture shock hits them hard, and they feel isolated and alone. The apartments that Cherry has found are adequate, but far apart from one another. They had not really realized how few people speak English, and now they are all worried about learning Chinese.

José calls them for a check-in conversation after two weeks and listens to all of their frustrations. He encourages them all to enroll in a language school course and tells them they should not think about the restaurant until they are more settled. Anil is not convinced; he wants to get going as soon as possible. José reiterates his view that language is important for long-term success.

After the call, José arranges for David and Cherry to meet the four Indian missionaries and worship together; he asks David and Cherry to see if there are ways that they can all encourage and support one another, and possibly even work together as a team. At this stage, however, he feels it is more important for them to get to know each other and have fellowship.

Jakob, Neesha, and Lal begin learning Chinese. Anil instead decides to focus on securing a location for the restaurant. The team meets with David and Cherry in a local hotel, and worship, pray and chat together.

José calls again one month after the team has arrived. He finds that the meeting with David and Cherry went well, that the team is now feeling more settled, and that Anil has decided not to enroll in a language school. He encourages them again that language is going to be important, but Anil doesn't change his mind. Still, now that the team is established, José contacts the church in India and encourages them to make contact as part of their member care responsibilities.

At the Walking Together office, Marcus gets a message from the Singaporean donors. They are open to investing in the restaurant idea, but they want to see a clear vision, strategy, and financial plan. Marcus passes the message on to Anil, together with samples of documents he has used in the past. He does not hear anything back.

SIX MONTHS

It's September. Jakob and Lal are doing well at language school; Neesha is struggling, but she perseveres. Jakob and Lal have managed to share the Gospel with two of their neighbors in their apartment block, and, with a mix of English and Chinese, meet to read the Bible once a week.

Anil has found a place for the restaurant but has still not written a plan for the investors. He's a good people person and a good cook, but writing this kind of document is not easy for him. Marcus calls him and Jakob up, gets them to send over what they have so far, and together they talk over how the idea is going to work. Based on their conversation and Anil's notes, Marcus writes up a plan and asks Anil to send it to Singapore.

The team continues to meet once a month with David and Cherry, and there's a growing sense that the six of them want to plant a church together. Jakob and Lal would like somewhere to invite their friends to, but David seems unsure.

José calls us the team one last time for a six-month check-in. He reviews the team's strategy and keeps them accountable to goals they set for this point. From now on, WT plans to shift the focus of their involvement from the team to the Indian church. He contacts the church, passes on the news from the team and encourages the church to take over with member care responsibility. With the church back in India now able to support, send and care for its missionaries, Walking Together's role in establishing the Kunming team is done.

However, José reminds them that he is available for further mentoring if they would like to make use of it, but stresses that their home church is now their main point of contact. Anil takes up José's offer of a regular mentoring appointment.

A HICCUP

With the money from Singapore, Anil rents premises for the restaurant and buys equipment. Neesha drops out of language school, claiming that she needs to help Anil get the restaurant set up, but this is just an excuse - privately, she has lost the desire to study any more. Jakob and Lal now have five friends that they are meeting with regularly to talk about the Bible. Anil and Neesha have had some conversations, but with limited Chinese, they have not been able to share their faith.

By December, the restaurant is up and running. The four missionaries cook and serve meals lunchtime and evenings, providing them a small income; on their days off, they try to share their faith with their neighbors. Jakob and Lal continue to have more success than Anil and Neesha, and Anil is getting frustrated by this.

Towards the end of the month, José gets an angry phone call from David. David is with a traditional mission agency but knows that José has been helping with oversight of the Indian missionaries. It turns out that David had invited Cherry and the Indian missionaries to meet up for a Christmas time of worship and fellowship together, at a hotel conference room booked in his name. But Jakob had decided that it would be a nice idea to bring his Chinese neighbors along for a Christmas service too. David is furious. Didn't Jakob know the security risks of bringing Chinese people to a place where foreigners were meeting?

José feels that this would be a good opportunity for the Indian church to learn more about the realities of missionary sending. So he does not contact the missionaries directly. Instead, he calls the church and explains the problem. They agree to encourage Jakob to be more careful, and to work things out with David. José also takes the opportunity to have a conversation with the church about security and crisis management policies; Faith will provide some sample policies, and help the church to tailor them to the situation in China. It is up to the church to communicate these with the missionaries on the field.

This incident has probably killed off any chance of the Indian missionaries planting a church together with David and Cherry, but José doesn't feel the need to intervene - Walking Together has handed over to the Indian church, and the missionaries on the field seem well on their way to planting a church already.

NOT FOR EVERYONE

It's August, and the team have been in China for nearly a year and a half. Jakob and Lal have been running a successful church plant in their apartment complex. Two members have got baptised. Anil has been having mentoring sessions with José once a month by Skype, and José is aware that things are not going well.

Although he would not say so to his home church, Anil is jealous of how Jakob is doing. Neesha is managing to pick up more of the language, but Anil has no local friends, finds communication difficult, and does not see his ministry developing. José has been encouraging him to keep going, to see himself as part of a team, and to try to find different kinds of opportunities for outreach. The church have also done a good job of praying for him, sending him encouragements and checking in with him. But it's no good; he's had enough. José quietly lets the church know that they may need to start thinking about a face-saving way to bring the couple home. They'll also going to need some training on how to do a re-entry debrief...

Once the church is prepared to receive Anil and Neesha back, José encourages them to plan ahead. There is the relationship with the Singaporean donors to manage, and there is Jakob and Lal's future to think about. For their part, they want to stay; they feel their ministry is going well, and that they are able to continue to run the restaurant. But since things have not worked out with David and Cherry, will they have enough opportunities for local fellowship and encouragement?

Well, as it happens, José has just heard about a young man from Nigeria who is interested in church planting in China. Let's hope he likes mustard oil...

WHAT MAKES A GOOD CATALYST TEAM?

This hypothetical situation has shown the possibilities of what a catalyst team might look like. We've seen how they network between churches, new missionaries, existing field situations, and other players in the mission world such as donors and training providers.

We've also seen how they work to resource churches, acting as 'incubators' to allow them to send missionaries and gradually increase their own capacity to send and support. In the same way that church planters have to provide a great deal of early input but over time gently encourage a church towards independence, catalysts also have to perform the same balancing act with respect to sending churches or other sending bodies: they aim towards having the church take responsibility for the field missionaries, but at the same time remain available to offer further advice or assistance when required.

Finally, we've seen that because catalysts are not the missionaries' "sending organisation", they can provide an external, third-party perspective. They can provide impartial assessments to churches or field situations, and may be able to hear from missionaries things that they would feel uncomfortable or afraid of saying to their supporting church because of the power dynamics involved.

For this to work well, a catalyst team will need to have the following characteristics:

- Most of all, excellent relational and networking skills.

- Cross-cultural sensitivity and awareness.

- Integrity, honesty and discretion; character required to be seen as an "honest broker".

- Strong knowledge and awareness of mission trends and activity within a given geographic area.

- Mentoring and member care skills.

- At least one team member with a specialism in finance, missional business, and fundraising.

- At least one team member with a specialism in training.

EXAMPLES IN PRACTICE

The mission catalyst idea is not completely new; there arc already a number of organisations which are responding to the emerging needs of mission movements in this kind of way. We will briefly highlight two examples of similar organisations.

ASIACMS

Asia CMS was founded in 2012 by Kang-San Tan and Loun Ling Lee. It sees its role explicitly in terms of connecting partners: churches, organisations and individuals. AsiaCMS operates as a broker for training and resources and as a facilitator of collaboration – rather than pursuing a specific goal of their own, it exists to serve and support the goals of others. Similarly, as an organisation, it has no mission partners of its own, but "co-sends" with others – local mission movements select and send, while AsiaCMS resources, trains and supports.

As Jonathan Ingleby explains in his book Storm Signals, AsiaCMS will have a centre but it will emphasise the independence and autonomy of partners... leadership will be local and will be shaped by dialogue rather than directives, so that the vision, shape and mission of the local leaders are not predetermined by outsiders. These local leaders can appeal for financial support, but only after they have articulated their vision for local mission. The centre's role would largely be to ensure that there were shared values. Full financial independence would be the goal and the time frame for achieving this would be brief... Thus the coordinating hub would be a "resource and training" hub... In general, mission structures would be kept to the minimum and the focus would be on building relationships, consultation and dialogue, all leading to local autonomy. After the initial partnership the hope would be that the independent local entity would appreciate, and want to continue with, the shared mission and vision, and also be able to find strength and value in the centre's training programmes.[1]

---

1.   Jonathan Ingleby, 2016, *Storm Signals*, Oxford: Regnum, 116-117.

At our Future of Mission Symposium in 2019, Loun Ling Lee gave some examples of AsiaCMS's partnerships and how they have realised these goals. For example, in their provision of training, rather than just bringing existing training "packages" into a new context, they would prefer to work with the partner organisation to develop appropriate material together, co-teach with the local partners to enable them to continue the teaching sustainably on their own, and also provide seed funding to enable them to develop their own training centres.

So to expand on Jonathan's last sentence, not only would local entities find strength and value from the partnership with AsiaCMS, but they would also become in a position to contribute capacity back to AsiaCMS in the future.

This idea of deliberately working as a collaboration and resource hub for external partners, of co-sending rather than having "our missionaries", and brokering connections between churches and organisations, all seems to me to be a concrete outworking of a networked model of mission that I have been exploring here. I think the AsiaCMS approach is a highly appropriate response to the world situation, and a pointer on the way to the question of "what next after agency?"

EUROPE COLLABORATION

A different style of mission catalyst is represented by Europe Collaboration, which seeks to connect "kingdom entrepreneurs" to enable church planting in Europe. Europe Collaboration acts as a broker between selected church planters and potential donors. In the past year, Europe Collaboration has fostered the planting of 12 churches across Europe.

Church planting proposals are referred to Europe Collaboration through partnerships of church planting networks and large churches. The proposals then go through a rigorous selection, interview and due diligence process, with a "business plan" for the selected proposal being forwarded to a network of donors to provide seed capital for the initial church plant.

The main emphasis of Europe Collaboration seems to be on the connection between church planters and donors in order to provide project-based financial support. This clearly implies that as catalysts they have a further focus beyond simply church planting in Europe; major donors are only required by church planting styles and models of church that involve high start-up costs and reliance on external resources, rather than "vulnerable mission" approaches which seek to utilize internal resources and reduce external dependency. However, as well as the financial relationship, Europe Collaboration connects the church planters it supports with experienced church planting specialists for ongoing advice, training and mentoring.

In that sense, Europe Collaboration fulfils many of the features of a mission catalyst we have described above, although one with more of a focus on the church plant as project and product rather than the church planter as person. On the one hand it demonstrates the growing trend towards a project- and outcomes-based understanding of mission, but on the other it provides another example of the network hub or broker organisational model, which facilitates collaborative external partnerships for mission rather than bringing people or projects into its own organisational umbrella.

SUMMARY

The relationship between churches and mission agencies has always been an uneasy one; increasingly churches have wanted greater ownership and involvement in global mission, while agencies have come to be seen as "taking" the best people (and funds) "away" from the church. As mission continues to grow in the global South, there is a desire for a new model of mission which does not concentrate the power in the hands of the mission agency but rather empowers and develops the sending power of churches, denominations and individuals. Bryan Knell has written of the need for the agency to become more of a "mission consultancy", serving the needs of the church in its approach to global mission.

The mission catalyst idea is a practical way to move away from parachurch-driven mission, while sharing the experience and knowledge of mission specialists. As befits a missionary community that is increasingly non-Western, it replaces an organisational approach to mission with a relational, network-based approach. As its name implies, the goal of the mission catalyst is not to "get the job done", but to equip and empower others, aiming at the multiplication of mission movements around the world.

3

Executive Summary

❧

CHAPTER NINE

Executive Summary

THEOLOGICAL AND MISSIOLOGICAL ASPECTS

- While mission today is "everywhere to everywhere", it is still important to challenge churches that mission must involve "moving out". Churches will want to do mission "across the street" and reach the unreached "from home", but the Bible shows a clear and persistent picture of witness as being done from the perspective of the guest and the foreigner, not from the host. The cross-cultural mandate flows from the nature of God.

- Mission is now primarily a non-Western enterprise, and this often means that majority world missionaries are ministering "from below", often to people of greater wealth, health or education. Western missionary models are not adequate to support these new missionaries.

- If we accept that mission is God's (*missio dei*) and that God is "missionary by His very nature", then participating in mission is the way that Christians experience God. If this is true, then the idea of a "career missionary" is hard to support. It suggests that some people are missionaries and some are not, when actually all Christians are called to be missionaries. The mission agency exists to support career missionaries, but a better approach would be to believe that all Christians are missionaries and work out how best to support them. How would our mission praxis shift if we genuinely saw *all* Christians as missionaries?

- Mission agencies practice "extraction evangelism": they take one or two people out from their church contexts, and bring them into a separate agency where their mission work happens. This is an example of the individualistic thinking of the Western model. In the same way as with extraction in church planting, it is hard for the impact of mission to spread through a church or network of churches.

- Another result of the mission agencies' "extraction evangelism" is that they have failed to reproduce themselves. Within WEC, we have planted one mission agency in Indonesia and helped to establish one in Nigeria, but in other parts of the world, the focus is more on *recruitment* than on *reproduction*. If we believe that all 2.2 billion Christians are called to be missionaries and that the church is called to be in mission, then we will need thousands and potentially millions of mission support structures to support them. Instead of bringing new members into the agency, we need instead to find ways of equipping churches and networks to be mission senders.

- Two hundred years ago when Carey set up the Western mission agency model, the formal institutional organisation (company, friendly society, etc.) was seen as the best way to organise individuals together for a common task. Now trust in institutions has declined.

The modern equivalent is the network or movement: informal associations without strong ideas of membership but with high feelings of ownership.

- Emerging non-Western mission movements value communication, relationship, and partnership much more than the Western model. Links are built between home churches, "field" churches, diaspora communities and like-minded organisations.

- Many of the functions of the mission agency are either now more generally available to the public than they were two hundred years ago (travel planning, international financial transfers), or have become available from external specialist providers (training, member care, health care). While some structural assistance is still needed, especially by those in the majority world, the core functions of an agency can now be seen as mobilization; candidate screening; ensuring that missionaries receive adequate training and development; providing mentoring and accountability; and team formation.

- Mission agencies have traditionally performed these functions *instead of* the church, bringing church members into the agency and organising them into a mission movement. In the future, mission agencies will instead need to perform these functions *in service of* the church, to help the church be more effective in mission.

- Agencies will therefore need to see themselves as existing to serve others rather than to drive their own agenda. In the case of SIL International, a shift from seeing mission in terms of "production" (what "we" do ourselves) to "impact" (what we see achieved) has helped to re-orient an agency around serving the needs of others, and help it to be generous with its resources - giving support externally, rather than purely serving its own members.

GLOBAL SHIFTS AND THEIR IMPACT

- The climate emergency will become increasingly established as the most important global trend. It will impact on mission in multiple areas: through the creation of climate refugees (forced migration), instability and wars due to competition for resources, non-viability of mission facilities (headquarters buildings, training centres, etc.) particularly in the majority world, and changing attitudes towards short-term international travel.

- Migration rates have largely held static at around 3% of the global population, but within that the number of forced migrants (refugees, asylum seekers and internally displaced peoples) has exploded recently. We can expect this trend to continue.

- The high number and relative openness of first-generation migrants means that a mission sender must think carefully about the most appropriate place to reach particular people groups. It should not automatically be assumed that the best place to reach Somalians, for example, is in Somalia. Outreach through diaspora or migrant communities should be considered as an alternative.

- Because of the large number of migrants and diaspora communities, mission sending structures must not assume a link between place and people group. There should not be an automatic assumption that missionary teams in Spain are there to reach the Spanish, nor that the best place to reach Turks is in Turkey. Networks which group missionaries in the same locality (even though possible working amongst different people groups) will need to be supplemented by networks to resources missionaries working with the same people group (though possibly in widely different places around the world).

- Post-liberalism and post-secularism are major world trends, and impact on mission in several different ways. Governments have learnt how to use toxic religion in the service of nationalism. For example, the Indian government's Hinduisation has already led to the persecution of Muslims (and, with the Citizenship Amendment Act, the implication that they are "not real Indians"), but we can anticipate similar moves being made against Christians. Nationalism and religious identity will increase distrust of foreign missionaries.

- However, some post-liberal governments are also co-opting Evangelical Christianity, in ways that are incredibly damaging to Gospel witness. Politically conservative British, Brazilian, American and Filipino missionaries will inevitably be seen through the lens of their home country governments. There is also the risk that nationalistic and isolationist tendencies will increase in Evangelical churches in these countries. This may lead to fewer missionaries going overseas, and lower cultural sensitivity amongst those missionaries who do go. Missionary recruitment will need to take this into account. Recruitment resources may be better spent in areas where Christianity is not a *de facto* state religion.

- Because of these trends, Evangelicals cannot afford to remain politically neutral or politically uneducated. Missionary education will need to develop missionaries' political awareness, both in terms of global issues and their own self-awareness of their worldview and the relationship between political worldview and Christianity.

- Post-Christianity is a reality in many parts of Europe, with many indigenous populations of Europe becoming functionally unreached. This should not have a major impact on missionary strategy as we are already assuming an "everywhere-to-everywhere" paradigm of mission. It should, however, be seen as a warning that the strongholds of Christianity are not fixed. There is a risk of similar post-Christianisation happening in other areas of the world which are currently considered Christian sending nations.

- One lesson we see from European Christianity is that Evangelicals have been relatively poor at transmitting their faith across generations. Family ministry should be regarded as an integral part of mobilization.

- The world is more urban and will become more so. Transculturism, also known as "global youth culture", makes it more attractive to recruit from and send to global cities. The cultural distance between global cities in different countries can now be lower than the cultural distance between cities and rural areas in the same country.

- Additionally, global cities are strategic places of missionary activity, both in terms of "sending" - as significant gatherings of Christians from many different countries - and "receiving" - as significant gatherings of non-Christians from many different countries. An appropriate response would be to develop missional hubs in places such as Manila, Cairo, Hanoi and Lagos both for mobilization and for ministry.

- More globally nomadic millenials should also be challenged to see themselves as cross-cultural missionaries, and support structures such as agencies should find ways to resource and equip them as such.

- As these millenials see themselves as culturally fluid global nomads, international mission agencies should celebrate their multicultural nature and provide a more globalised experience for these millenials by organising their orientation and short-term programmes along regional or global lines instead of national lines.

- In general, the world is getting older; life expectancy is increasing and population pyramids are shifting more towards working-age and older people. This is already evident in Europe and countries like Japan, but will become a global trend. Mission to and by the older generation will need to be factored into current strategies.

SHIFTS IN CHRISTIANITY

- More than half of both the worldwide Church and the missionary community are now from the Global

South, while missionary sending from traditional areas such as Europe, North America and (to a degree) Korea is declining. Models of mission established to serve the Global North are not necessarily fit for the Global South.

- Majority world Christianity is predominantly "enthusiastic" - Pentecostal and charismatic - with a priority of spiritual and charismatic decision-making and the human encounter, instead of systematic organisational structures. Within WEC we are well equipped to be compatible with this, but it raises issues working and partnering across cultures.

- At this time, we have not seen any truly distinctive mission structures arising from the Global South. Most have broadly followed patterns that they have inherited from the Global North.

- There are some distinctives to Global South mission, however. There is often a greater feeling of "family connection" between home church and remote ministry - which can express itself as a pressure to replicate home denominational structures overseas. Mission is often done using local rather than imported resources (sometimes termed "vulnerable mission"). There are entrepreneurial attitudes to financial support. Commitment is long-term, with high expectations around training and involvement, and the ministry is normally centered around church planting and evangelism.

- Both majority world missions movements and minority world missions bring their own strategic objectives - for example, while Europe-based missions focus on Africa for reasons of colonial heritage, many African missions have a vision for the re-evangelisation of Europe. It is important to see these visions as complementary, not competitive.

- Developing partnerships with emerging missions movements outside of our organisation can be beneficial for both, but needs to be done on the basis of mutual respect and with sensitivity to power imbalances.

- To effectively welcome majority world participants within our organisation, we need ways of listening to (and taking seriously) their voices, hopes and experiences. New members who have not yet been "indocrinated" into organisational realities can help us see where our processes do not work for them. What are our mechanisms for this?

- From the first days of the church, the Gospel has spread across people groups through the witness of migrants and refugees. Based on UN migration data, we can estimate that there are at least 16 million Evangelical Christians living outside of their home countries.

- Diaspora church communities can often be more committed to evangelism than their home-country equivalents. For example, in Taiwan Christians make up 2% of the population, while 25-30% of Taiwanese in the US are Christian and two-thirds are converts.

- Diaspora ministry can be categorised into five aspects: mission *to* diaspora (external missionaries ministering to a migrant people group); mission *through* diaspora (migrants ministering to others of the same people group); mission *across* diaspora (migrants minis-

tering to other diaspora groups in the same country);
mission *beyond* diaspora (migrants ministering to the
majority people group); and mission *from* diaspora (migrants ministering to those in their home country).

- Of these five aspects, the first two are well established. Many African churches in the UK are attempting to move into mission beyond diaspora, but have
only seen significant success in mission through or
across diaspora. More mobilization and support could
be provided to encourage diaspora churches to reach
out beyond and from their communities.

- However, attitudes of traditional agencies towards
diaspora churches need to change. Many of these churches
are well-established in terms of their theology, resources,
training, and their expectations and visions for mission.
They are not blank canvases, available for us to paint on
our mission strategies. We need to display the humility
to serve their purposes, accept their leadership, and
work to their agenda. If residual attitudes can be overcome, building partnerships and seconding missionaries to diaspora churches can be advantageous for both
sides.

TECHNOLOGY

- The majority of the world's population are now
connected to the Internet, and this percentage will continue to increase. Technological advances and increased
connectedness allows for new possibilities for discipleship and evangelism.

- In the past, missionary activity has often been a driver for creating new technologies. Now, the balance has shifted from development to use of technology. More consideration should be given to how mission could benefit from technologies which are not currently available.

- Mission agencies and ministries such as Sat7 have shown themselves to be effective at using media channels and targeted online advertising to connect with seekers and follow up with contacts. However, this needs to be coupled with local connections where possible.

- Online discipleship and mentoring is now a possibility, although questions need to be answered about language and cultural sensitivity.

- Anyone can develop and launch online evangelism and discipleship activities from anywhere in the world. However, coordination between these remote developers and on-the-ground missionaries, churches and pastors is often lacking. There is a key co-ordinating role for connecting the needs and experience of field workers with the ingenuity and resources of "digital missionaries".

- There is also an important role for developing online seeker and discipleship communities. Most "digital evangelism" and discipleship is done on an individualistic, one-on-one model. It is important to build platforms for community engagement, both purely virtually and also relating to physical communities in specified geographical areas.

FINANCE

  - The expectation that missionaries are full-time and
fully-funded from churches overseas has multiple problems. It cements a distinction between "professional"
missionaries and other Christians who are not regarded
as missionaries, and it is not accessible for the increasing number of cross-cultural missionaries from the majority world.

  - Business as mission is one way to allow missionaries to self-support and gain access to mission fields, but
requires a very high level of commitment and enterpreneurial spirit. It should not be regarded as the only
approach.

  - Smaller-scale income generation models such as
those being investigated by Acts18 should be encouraged. Time and effort spent developing new models of
support can enable many more workers to be active in
cross-cultural ministry.

  - As international organisations with contacts around
the world, agencies should investigate setting up online
casual work businesses as ways to provide income for
cross-cultural workers.

  - However, for many, the only realistic way to access
and maintain a life in another country will be as a migrant worker, international student or similar. Indeed,
doing so can be a better way to develop natural networks of relationships. Mission organisations should
allow for these possibilities in all countries, not just
creative access nations.

- Of course, many mission-minded Christians already are active as migrant workers and international students. Once we accept that "traditional" missionaries can live and work in these roles, it becomes harder to make a distinction between them and "non-missionaries" working overseas.

- Therefore, our organisations should both allow for a variety of approaches to income and support, and should also be structurally flexible in terms of membership to include those living and working cross-culturally in a variety of capacities.

- Teams should be trained explicitly to be accommodating of different financial models and levels of commitment and availability. If not handled carefully, this can lead to unrealistic expectations and tensions between team members.

HOLISTIC SUGGESTIONS

- As mentioned above, growing world mission through replication is a key strategy for engaging the whole church in mission, not just an "elite" mission force. However, there is still a role for professionals in providing support and mentoring to establish new mission structures.

- Our agencies and sending structures need to take a much more positive approach to "non-missionaries". Intentionally resourcing and equipping migrant workers, international students, and diaspora churches would vastly increase the number of cross-cultural mission workers even if they are outside of our organisational boundaries.

- Concepts of membership should be sufficiently flexible to support a "movement" model rather than an "organisation" model. In areas where security is a consideration, this will require negotiation. But new approaches to funding and an appreciation of the missionary call on every Christian means that we should consider membership models which are "porous" (easily passing in and out), based on "centered sets" rather than "bounded sets". We should allow for partnerships with like-minded Christians which are flexible in terms of commitment, involvement and timescale.

- Branches may consider having a closed "inner" membership and an open "outer" membership.

- Rather than recruiting from churches into mission agencies, the focus should be on developing partnerships with churches and networks of churches; envisioning them for mission; encouraging them to find appropriate missional roles for all of their members; and then empowering, training, and resourcing them to support these roles. This support provided by an external "mission catalyst" will decrease over time as these churches and networks mature into mission senders, either autonomously or as part of a global missions network.

- I would encourage greater mission engagement with non-Christian diaspora groups, similar to the Neighbours Worldwide model. This would preferably be done by missionaries who are also "foreign" to the country of service, as maintaining the "guest perspective" is both missiologically important and allows for shared experiences between the missionary and unreached person.

- Agencies in the traditional model such as ours should ensure that they are structured sufficiently to support missionaries from country A working in country B to reach people from country C.

- Agencies should also be encouraged to engage with diaspora Christian communities. This should be done with awareness and sensitivity that many diaspora churches already have a well-developed mission plan. Where there is such a mission plan, missionaries should be encouraged to serve diaspora churches, partnering with them to assist with their mission goals; where cross-cultural mission is less prominent, missionaries should be encouraged to mobilize them for mission.

- Where cross-cultural mission goals align, it may make sense to encourage missionaries planting a new church to partner with local Christian communities as much as possible. Even in a "unreached area," there may be other resources to work with, and doing so involves more people in mission.

- Diaspora and migrant non-Christian communities should be seen not just in terms of evangelism and church planting, but as an opportunity for early mobilization - both to other nearby ethnic groups, and, where appropriate, challenged to be witnesses to their own ethnic group in "home" countries.

- Similarly, each ministry context should be seen as a mobilization context. Where there are new churches formed through missionary activity, they should be involved in cross-cultural ministry at an early stage. Where there are other churches in the area, particularly those of another ethnic group, they should be mobilized for ministry. The concept of the missionary as catalyst should always raise the question "Who else can we involve?"

- We should invest in teams placed in strategic global cities to network between churches of different ethnicities for mobilization and cross-cultural ministry.

- A catalytical opportunity is also found in boundary people groups, where unreached people are in close proximity with large populations of Evangelical Christians. Identifying and researching these areas, and partnering with local churches to determine what support (if any) would help them to reach their neighbours.

- Training, orientation, and short-term mission programmes should be offered on a regional rather than national basis to emphasise the multicultural nature of the mission for "global nomad" generations.

- None of these measures will be effective without the rise of a global prayer network for missions. WEC's own prayer groups are demographically limited. We need to challenge every church to develop a prayer passion for the unreached.

SUMMARY CONCLUSIONS

- As a mission, we need to shift from *production thinking* to *impact thinking*, from *recruitment* to *reproducibility*, and consider how we mobilize and equip the *whole Church* for mission.

- One major way to do this will be to raise up teams, outside of our church planting structures and possibly outside of our organisational structure entirely, to develop catalytic partnerships with churches and church groups to help develop their sending capacity, with a particular focus on the vibrant global South missions movement.

- Another way to shift focus from production to impact is to envisage every ministry context as an opportunity for training and mobilization. With the world now made up of a mosaic of reached and unreached people alongside one another, spending time mobilizing, training and supporting local Christian communities to become engaged in cross-cultural work can be a more effective way to plant churches than doing the work directly. Missionaries should see their role as primarily catalytical, not ministerial.

- A third way is to look for areas where inter-agency and inter-organisational connection and collaboration would increase missionary effectiveness. Facilitating these connections is a way to increase impact for everyone. One such area is the connection between field situations and technological pioneers, to ensure that mission-focused technologies are well suited to the needs of church planters on the ground.

- Structurally, within the organisation, we must put into practice what we believe about mission being "from everywhere to everywhere." All branches should be considered trans-national branches, sharing information and fellowship across those working with the same people group in different parts of the world. All ministry branches should be prepared to recruit and accept teams reaching whatever people groups are present in their area.